CSI | for the First Responder

A Concise Guide

CSI | for the First Responder

A Concise Guide

Jan LeMay

 CRC Press
Taylor & Francis Group
Boca Raton   London   New York

CRC Press is an imprint of the
Taylor & Francis Group, an **informa** business

CRC Press
Taylor & Francis Group
6000 Broken Sound Parkway NW, Suite 300
Boca Raton, FL 33487-2742

© 2011 by Taylor and Francis Group, LLC
CRC Press is an imprint of Taylor & Francis Group, an Informa business

Library of Congress Cataloging-in-Publication Data

LeMay, Jan.
CSI for the first responder : a concise guide / Jan LeMay.
p. cm.
Includes bibliographical references and index.
ISBN 978-1-4398-1922-7 (pbk. : alk. paper)
1. Crime scene searches. 2. Criminal investigation. 3. First responders. I. Title.

HV8073.L4165 2011
363.25'2--dc22

2010040821

Visit the Taylor & Francis Web site at
http://www.taylorandfrancis.com

and the CRC Press Web site at
http://www.crcpress.com

I would like to thank Sheriff John Cooke and the Weld County Sheriff's Office for all of your trust, support, and investment in me over the years.

This book is dedicated to my wife, Georgia. Your strength and determination motivate me, your kindness and compassion inspire me, and the love you demonstrate to everyone in your life moves me. You are my greatest blessing.

Table of Contents

Preface   **xi**
Introduction   **xiii**
About the Author   **xvii**

1   Crime Scene Approach   **1**

What Is a Crime Scene?   1
Securing the Scene   1
Rendering Aid   2
Establishing a Perimeter   3
Legal Considerations to Search and Seizure   4
Scene Assessment   6
Scene Search   7

2   Crime Scene Documentation   **9**

Photography   10
Video   11
Sketching   12
    Title box   14
    Legend   15
    Floor plan   15
    Elevation diagram   16
    Exploded diagram   16
    Perspective diagram   16
Methods of Measurement   18
    Rectangular coordinates   19
    Triangulation   19
    Transecting baseline   19
    Azimuth or polar coordinates   20
Notes and Reports   21
Collecting Evidence   23
Process for Latent Prints   24
Chain of Custody   24

3   Evidence   27

What Is Evidence?   27
Direct Evidence   27
Indirect Evidence   27
Class Characteristics   28
Individual Characteristics   28

4   Biological Evidence   31

Scene Safety   31
Inhalation   31
Ingestion   32
Absorption   32
Injection   32
Searching for Biological Evidence   33
Documentation   34
Collection   34
Trace DNA   37
General Collection Tips   38
Presumptive Tests   38
Sexual Assault Kits   39
Combined DNA Indexing System (CODIS)   39
Elimination Samples   40

5   Trace Evidence   41

Hair   43
Fibers   44
Accelerants   44
Wood   45
Soil   45
Glass   46
Plant Material and Seeds   46
Metals   47
Paint   48

6   Impression Evidence   49

Two-Dimensional Impressions   50
Documenting Two-Dimensional Impressions   52
Collecting Two-Dimensional Impressions   52
Three-Dimensional Impressions   54
Documenting Three-Dimensional Impressions   55

Choosing the Right Scale   58
Casting Three-Dimensional Impressions   59
Tire Impressions, Special Considerations   61
Tool Marks   62
Databases and Other Investigative Aids   63

7   Firearms Evidence   67

Safety   67
Understanding Firearms   68
Caliber   68
Rifling   69
Individual Characteristics on Bullets   70
Shell Casings   70
Shotguns, Shells, and Wadding   72
National Integrated Ballistics Information Network (NIBIN)   72
Gunshot Residue   74
Handling, Unloading, and Packaging Firearm Evidence   75

8   Documents   79

Handwriting   79
Typewriters   80
Computer Printers   83
Paper and Ink Analysis   84
Indented Writing   85
Collection and Preservation   85

9   Fingerprints   87

Patent Impressions   88
Latent Impressions   88
Plastic Impressions   90
Searching for Fingerprints   90
Developing and Lifting Fingerprints   91
Photographing Fingerprints   95
Automated Fingerprint Identification System (AFIS)   95
Porous Items   97

10   Controlled Substances   99

Documentation   99
Drug Identification   101
Field Tests   108
Prescription Drug Identification   111

11 Death Scene Investigation   **113**

Cause and Manner of Death   114
Jurisdiction over the Body   115
Postmortem Lividity   116
Rigor Mortis   117
Scene Documentation   118
Law Enforcement's Role at Autopsy   119

12 Courtroom Presentation and Testimony   **121**

Preparation and Pretrial Conference   121
Courtroom Dress and Demeanor   123
Courtroom Exhibits and Displays   124
Adversarial System   125

13 Case Studies   **127**

Case Number 1   127
Case Number 2   130
Case Number 3   134
Case Number 4   138

Index   **143**

Preface

It has been my experience that many law enforcement officers in agencies large and small are responsible for processing crime scenes. In some large agencies the first responders may simply secure the scene and call for a crime scene investigator (CSI) to process it. But in many agencies the first responder is expected to also be the CSI. The purpose of this book is to provide first responders with a practical and instructional resource that will guide them through the documentation, collection, and preservation of most types of evidence that they may encounter. It covers all aspects of the crime scene investigation, from the approach to the scene, securing the scene, searching and identifying evidence, documenting the evidence by means of notes and reports, photography and videotape, sketches and diagrams, and collection and preservation of the evidence. It also explains the investigative value of different types of evidence so the reader understands why each type of evidence may be important to cases. And this book will provide the reader with some valuable information on presenting evidence in court and tips for providing testimony. The courtroom is where law enforcement work is really put to the test and I believe that most law enforcement officers receive little or no training and instruction on courtroom testimony.

The final chapter of the book features case studies. It provides real-life examples where the techniques described in the book are implemented. There are cases presented where first responders did an excellent job at scene security and documentation, and some cases where some simple mistakes were made and how those mistakes could have been avoided and how they were overcome. Each case presents highlights of the real-life lessons learned from the experiences and is not simply the telling of "war stories." The cases are interesting and applicable examples of the lessons taught in the book.

Additionally, the book includes a "Quick Reference Guide" on a CD in PDF format. Most first responders have laptop computers in their cars. This digital version of the "Quick Reference Guide" can be downloaded to that computer and can easily be referenced. The guide can also be printed and kept in a pocket or notepad. When encountering evidence you are unfamiliar with, you can easily look it up in the guide and learn how to document, collect, and preserve it. This easily referenced resource can be with you at all times.

Introduction

A story I was once told by a district attorney shocked me. A man walking down the street late at night witnessed a man break a window at an electronics store and enter the store through the broken window. The witness called the police, who responded promptly to find the suspect climbing out of the broken window carrying a television set. Caught red-handed, the suspect was taken into custody and charged with burglary. He pleaded not guilty and took his case to trial. Despite the witness's and police officers' identification of the defendant, the jury found the defendant not guilty.

The prosecutor, baffled by the verdict, set up an interview session with the jurors. He asked where he went wrong with the case and why their deliberations resulted in a not guilty verdict. The jury foreman spoke up and said, "If you would have had DNA evidence, we would have convicted him."

Today, popular television shows and movies have put crime scene investigation, physical evidence, and forensic science in the forefront of the public conscious. Due to these shows the public has what many consider an unrealistic perception of what law enforcement and forensic science is truly capable of. Some refer to this as the "*CSI* effect." The expectation is that there is a lot of physical evidence at every crime scene, the crime scene investigator will find it almost effortlessly, and that forensic analysis of the evidence will solve the crime—every time.

Although this expectation is unrealistic, it is true that most crime scenes will yield some physical evidence. A crime scene must be rendered safe, secured, and searched properly. Once evidence is identified, the evidence must be properly documented, collected, and preserved. This is a tremendous responsibility for individuals placed in the position of crime scene investigation. And very often, all of this responsibility falls on the shoulders of just one individual, the first responder. Some law enforcement agencies have the luxury of having officers who can respond to a scene and secure it, then call for assistance from a crime lab, or other officers with specialized training in crime scene processing. But many law enforcement agencies lack the manpower and resources to have individuals dedicated to the important task of crime scene investigation. The first responder also has the roles of crime scene investigator, evidence technician, and detective.

This is a great responsibility to be sure, but crime scene processing can be performed effectively and efficiently with the acquisition and application of some simple skills. Crime scene investigation is not an art that requires some innate talent. It is the application of a series of skill sets that can be acquired through some education and practice. Anyone who learns these skills and applies them with common sense can become a very proficient crime scene investigator. Through practice and experience it can become easy for the first responder to find, identify, document, and preserve physical evidence that may be overlooked by a less learned investigator. This can result in more identifications of suspects, more convictions, greater job satisfaction, and ultimately a safer public.

In 1910 in the city of Lyons, France, a young scientist named Edmond Locard (Figure I.1) convinced the police department that he could use science to help solve crimes. The police gave him two rooms in the attic and two assistants with whom to work. This is believed to be the world's first crime lab. Locard had a concept referred to as Locard's exchange principle. This principle states that whenever two items come into contact there is an exchange of material from one to the other. This has become a guiding principle in crime scene investigation.

When people commit crimes they may leave myriad evidence of their presence at the scene, everything from footwear impressions, tire impressions, hair, fingerprints, clothes or clothing fibers, blood, semen, saliva, even naturally shed skin cells. They may also take with them evidence of their presence. Some possibilities are carpet or fabric fibers, microscopic shards of broken glass, soil, plant material, metal fragments, blood and hair from the victim, or, of course, stolen goods. Sometimes this evidence is easy for the first responder to find; other times it takes some effort. But with a little knowledge and due diligence the evidence can be found. Once identified, its proper documentation, collection, and preservation may prove to be the key

Figure I.1 Edmond Locard (1877–1966).

in a successful investigation, arrest, and prosecution. The first responder is the key figure and is the most important person at a crime scene.

Second, I would like to emphasize that this book should serve only as a guide. No book could possibly have all of the answers for every situation. If ever a first responder has a question or concern over what is the best way to document and collect physical evidence, the best resource is the local crime lab. Don't be reluctant to call and speak to the analyst who will actually be examining the evidence. Most analysts will be happy to spend a few minutes on the phone with you to ensure that the evidence sent to the lab for analysis is going to be the best possible evidence.

About the Author

Jan LeMay has worked in law enforcement for seventeen years. He has served as a corrections officer and patrol officer, but the majority of his service has been spent working in a crime lab as a crime scene specialist and criminalist. He has experience at hundreds of crime scenes and dozens of homicide investigations.

LeMay is a member of a number of professional organizations including the International Association for Identification (IAI), the Rocky Mountain Division of the IAI (RMDIAI), the UK Fingerprint Society, the Canadian Identification Society, and the Colorado Forensic Footwear Information Network. He has served on the Forensic Photography Certification Board for the IAI and is a past president of the RMDIAI. He is board certified through the IAI as a crime scene analyst, forensic photographer, latent print examiner, and footwear examiner.

LeMay is an instructor at the Southern Institute of Forensic Science and the Weld County Law Enforcement Training Academy. He has instructed hundreds of students and law enforcement professionals in crime scene examination and documentation techniques. He has published numerous articles in law enforcement and has published numerous research projects and case studies in peer-reviewed forensic science journals.

Crime Scene Approach 1

What Is a Crime Scene?

Crime scene is a term we hear or use almost every day. But what is a crime scene? A crime scene is often defined as the location where a crime occurred. But a crime scene may also be any subsequent location that contains evidence of the crime. In many cases there is a primary crime scene where the crime actually occurred, and there may be numerous other locations that contain evidence. The vehicle that transported the suspects to and from the scene may contain evidence. The roadways traveled by the suspect after the crime where evidence may have been thrown out of a vehicle window while fleeing the scene should be considered a crime scene. The suspect's home should be considered a crime scene. It is where stolen goods, the clothes he or she was wearing during the crime, burglary tools, weapons, or other evidence may be found. Trash dumpsters or other disposal sites where evidence may have been discarded may also be considered crime scenes. The initial focus of the investigation is most often the primary crime scene. But it is important for the first responder to consider other possible locations that may need to be secured and searched.

A crime scene may be very small and confined in nature. The scene may be the backseat of a car where a sexual assault occurred. It may be just one room in a house. It may also be broad in scope. It may be an entire house or business ransacked by burglars. Or it may be miles of roadway where evidence was tossed out of a car. It may be the middle of a busy intersection. First responders must be open-minded and considerate of all possibilities when defining the scope of the crime scene they are searching.

Securing the Scene

The earliest stages of the crime scene investigation may be the most critical. How the officer initially approaches and secures the scene sets the tone for the rest of the crime scene investigation. A careless and haphazard approach may result in the loss or destruction of evidence. It may result in the distortion of the scene beyond what may be considered acceptable. For example, first responders may drive their vehicle over tire impressions left behind by the suspect vehicle. They may walk in the suspect's footsteps or handle door-knobs or light switches that may have been handled by the suspect. Although it may be impossible for first responders to prevent such things as leaving their own footwear impressions at a scene, it is imperative that they con-sider where the suspect may have walked and objects the suspect may have touched and make every effort to avoid those areas of contact.

The first responders' first responsibility at a crime scene must be that of safety. They must be aware of the possibility of suspect(s) still being present at the scene. If a search of the scene must be conducted for safety reasons the first responders must still be aware of the possibility of the destruction of physical evidence during that search and make efforts to prevent it, but their first responsibility must be to render the scene safe before any other investi-gation may proceed.

In addition to human threats at crime scenes, officers must consider other not so obvious threats to their safety. Biological hazards may be pres-ent at any type of crime scene. Every case from simple theft scenes or bur-glary scenes where a suspect cut himself, or, of course, assault or murder scenes may pose health hazards to the first responders. Dangerous booby traps are not uncommon hazards encountered at clandestine drug labs, not to mention the chemicals, fumes, and manufactured drugs themselves. First responders must be aware and alert for these types of hazards and take mea-sures to protect themselves when they are identified.

Rendering Aid

Once the scene is deemed to be safe it the responsibility of the first responder to render aid to any individuals on scene in need. Sometimes this cannot be accomplished without the distortion of the scene. Crime scene distortion is often unavoidable and acceptable in many cases where aid must be rendered. Distortion occurs when the scene is changed from its original appearance. It must not be confused with crime scene contamination. If a victim is moved from a bed to a floor to perform CPR (cardiopulmonary resuscitation), or furniture is moved out of the way to make room for a gurney, or a weapon is moved or secured to get it out of the way of emergency medical personnel, this is considered distortion. It does not necessarily destroy physical evidence and is necessary to provide aid to individuals at the scene, and therefore is not considered contamination. If first responders approach a scene by walk-ing up a dirt driveway, it is impossible for them to avoid leaving their own footwear impressions. As long as they are careful not to track over any other footwear impressions this is considered crime scene distortion and naturally is unavoidable.

If aid is being rendered to individuals at the scene, and objects are being moved within the scene, it is imperative that those actions are noted and documented. There must be explanations as to why items were moved, their condition prior to being moved, who moved them, and where they were moved to. If possible, it is recommended that the first responder take some quick photographs of items in their original locations prior to being moved. Just a few quick snapshots taken before the scene is distorted may help answer questions down the road as to the original appearance of the scene.

When aid is being rendered it is also the duty of the first responding officer to attempt to limit the number of emergency medical personnel who enter the crime scene. It may be acceptable to allow a limited number of medics in the scene and keep other nonessential personnel out. For example, if there is one assault victim in a home there is no need for ten firefighters to enter the scene and increase the chances of scene distortion or contamination.

Establishing a Perimeter

If the incident is of a nature that the first responder will be requesting assistance at the scene from other personnel, it may be necessary to establish perimeters around the scene. A perimeter may be established by simply removing all individuals from the scene and closing a door. It may be necessary to surround the scene with yellow barrier tape. In some cases it may be as simple as telling the property owners that you will be processing the scene for physical evidence and asking that they remain clear of the area until you are finished.

Larger, more complex scenes may require the establishment of both an inner perimeter and an outer perimeter. The inner perimeter is the perimeter around the actual crime scene. Only individuals who will be processing the scene are allowed into the inner perimeter. A scene entry log should be maintained at the inner perimeter to record the names of all individuals who enter the inner perimeter. In addition, the date, time, and purpose for their entry should be recorded as well (see Figure 1.1).

Anyone who enters the inner perimeter should report on his or her actions and observations within the crime scene. If the individual deemed it necessary to enter the scene, it is important that he or she write a report explaining why and describe his or her actions and observations.

An outer perimeter may also be established in some cases. The outer perimeter may be as simple as placing a patrol unit at both ends of the block to keep unnecessary personnel from approaching the scene and creating distractions or chaos near the scene. It may be permissible to allow other law enforcement personnel or residents on the street into the outer perimeter, but prohibit all others such as curious citizens and the press.

CRIME SCENE ENTRY LOG				
Case #:		Location:		Date:
DATE	TIME ENTERED	TIME EXITED	NAME	PURPOSE
COMPLETED BY:				

Figure 1.1 An example of a crime scene entry log.

It is a good practice to establish the perimeter farther out than you think is necessary. It is easy to scale back a perimeter if it is later determined that it would be acceptable. It is much more difficult to move a perimeter farther out after it has originally been established. If it is discovered that the scene is more expansive than originally thought, then it may be necessary to move vehicles and people back, which can create problems with scene security and result in scene distortion or contamination.

Figure 1.2 is a crime scene diagram of a shooting scene. Two victims standing in the east doorway of the trailer were shot. The first responders assumed that the shots came from the driveway east of the trailer. They established a perimeter by placing yellow barrier tape across the entrance to the driveway. Medical personnel and other law enforcement personnel responded to the scene, drove through the intersection, and drove over the shell casings, which had been ejected from the shooter's firearm. Many of the shell casings were damaged by the vehicles, and it is possible that some may have been lost due to the traffic. Had the first responder set the perimeter farther out, then that evidence may have been better preserved.

Legal Considerations to Search and Seizure

Once a scene is secured, and there is no longer any exigency to enter the scene, first responders must consider the legal ramifications of their presence

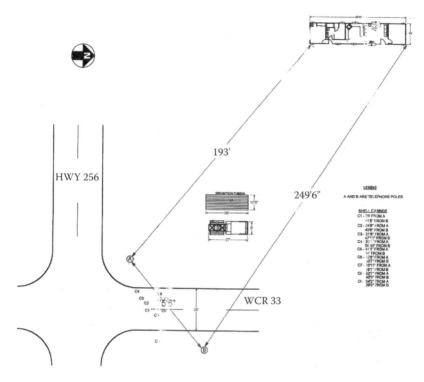

Figure 1.2 A diagram of a shooting scene. Shell casings near the intersection of the roadways were driven over by additional responders to the scene.

at the scene. The Fourth Amendment to the U.S. Constitution protects citizens from unreasonable search and seizure. This protection applies not just to their homes, but to their cars, boats, papers and effects, sheds and barns, offices, and other structures. If the scene is a burglary, it may only be necessary for first responders to explain to the property owner what steps they plan on taking to process the scene and ask for oral permission. In other types of incidents, such as a death investigation, it may be necessary to obtain written consent to search or a search warrant.

One consideration when obtaining consent is that the property owner may limit consent. The property owner may tell you it is alright for you to search the house, but prohibit you from entering the garage. Consent may also be withdrawn at any time. If the first responder is permitted by a property owner to search and later the property owner becomes uncomfortable with the search, he or she can withdraw that consent at any time and ask the officer to stop searching and even leave the property.

Any evidence seized during an illegal search will most likely be dismissed by the court and could jeopardize the case. The first responder must consider whether it is necessary or reasonable to require a signed consent form or a search warrant under the circumstances of the case. Whenever first responders have questions or concerns about the legality of a search they should consult with their local district attorney's office prior to conducting a crime scene search.

Scene Assessment

Once the crime scene is deemed safe and secured and the necessary steps have been taken to ensure a legal search, an assessment of the scene is conducted. This begins with a preliminary walk-through of the scene. This is not a scene search but is conducted to simply get a feel for the scene and determine how to proceed with processing the scene. During this walk-through an attempt to identify perishable or transitory evidence should be performed. Some types of evidence, if not acted upon immediately, may be lost or destroyed and the opportunity to document and collect them may be lost also. For example, if it is an outdoor scene with footwear impressions in snow, and it is a bright sunny day, it may be determined that the footwear impressions should be processed first before the snow melts and the footwear impressions are lost.

The author experienced a murder case where there was a greeting card on a hallway floor in the residence where the crime occurred. Resting on top of the greeting card was one lone hair. It was deemed that the hair was transitory in nature, as the simple act of walking past it could have caused the hair to move off of the card and never be relocated. So the first thing documented and collected at that scene was that hair.

During the initial walk-through the first responder should also consider the weather and lighting conditions. Evidence at an outdoor scene may be jeopardized if the weather conditions are turning foul. It may be prudent to wait to search and process an outdoor scene at night until the sun comes up. Searching and processing a scene in the dark can easily result in evidence being missed or accidentally destroyed when it is not seen in the dark.

First responders also need to assess the safety of the scene, consider biological hazards or other safety considerations, and take the necessary steps to protect themselves and others. They need to consider the status of personnel at the scene and ask, "Is this the type of scene I can process alone or do I need assistance?" This is a good time to also assess the scene security. Determine if the perimeter and the security established are going to be sufficient or if improvements need to be made.

Also, interview the reporting party and find out where they have walked in the scene, what they have touched or moved, and what they have observed in the scene. The reporting party or property owner is familiar with the property and can inform the first responder as to what is out of place and what is missing.

Scene Search

The first responder must take a systematic approach to searching crime scenes. A search conducted in a cursory or haphazard fashion may result in evidence being overlooked. A planned approach should be taken and the scene searched thoroughly.

The search should begin by inspecting the approach to and from the scene. A careful search for footwear and tire impressions should be conducted following the paths into and out of the scene.

Next, a careful inspection of the points of entry and egress into the scene should be conducted. These are often the best locations to find physical evidence at a crime scene. A careful inspection of the ground around the points of entry and egress should be conducted for footwear impressions. If a door was kicked in, footwear impressions may be found on the door itself. If a window was broken, a careful inspection for blood should be conducted as the suspect may have accidentally cut himself or herself while breaking the window or reaching in through it. The points of entry and egress should also be carefully inspected for fingerprints, hairs, fibers, tool marks, abandoned tools, and anything else the suspect might have left behind.

After the points of entry and exit have been thoroughly searched, a thorough search of the scene interior can be conducted. All who are participating in this search should follow a common path through the scene as to limit the chances of disturbing the scene. If the first responder chooses to have the property owner accompany him or her during the search to point out what has been disturbed or is missing, it should be made clear that the property owner should follow the first responder and try not to touch anything.

Notes should be taken as to the general condition of the scene. Is it neat or in disarray? Are lights on or off, are windows and doors open or closed, locked or unlocked?

It is vitally important that a crime scene is searched and examined with other senses besides sight. In addition to searching with their eyes, first responders should search with their nose and observe if there are any odors in the scene such as tobacco smoke, cologne or perfume, burnt gunpowder, gasoline, food or beverages, or any others that are detected. Any sounds should be noted such as music, televisions, washing machines, dishwashers, fans, or any other sounds detected in the scene. The absence of any odors or sounds should also be noted. Although it may be important to note what is observed, it may be equally as important and relevant to note what is not observed.

Crime Scene Documentation

2

It is crucial that crime scenes are documented thoroughly. First responders must be complete in documenting all of their observations at the scene. If the scene and evidence within the scene are not documented completely and clearly it may leave first responders and the evidence open to challenges in court. This may result in evidence being dismissed, which could have resulted in a successful prosecution, and damage the reputation and credibility of the first responders.

Even incidents that may appear to be noncriminal should be thoroughly documented. First responders should avoid the mindset that because an incident is noncriminal they will never be required to testify in court about the scene, and their observations and actions. Any incident has the potential for some sort of civil litigation. An incident of accidental death, while not a criminal investigation, may result in civil litigation between victims' families, employers, insurance companies, equipment manufactures, and so forth. Every scene first responders are called to may have the potential need for physical evidence and testimonial evidence to be presented in a court of law.

Crime scene documentation entails a number of key elements:*

- Notes
- Photographs/video
- Sketches
- Reports

Each singular element is vitally important and none are a substitute for the other. A description of an item of evidence in the officer's notes, photographs of that item of evidence, and a sketch of the scene depicting where that item of evidence was located, all together form a complete image of that physical evidence. It is a great benefit when introducing evidence in court to be able to describe an item of evidence and the condition in which it was found. Show photographs of the evidence as it was found. And then point to a diagram and show where it was found. The court and jurors will then have a more thorough understanding of the value of that evidence. Avoid the

---

* Ross M. Gardner, *Practical Crime Scene Processing and Investigation* (Boca Raton, FL: CRC Press, 2005).

mindset of "I took lots of good pictures, so why do I need to describe every-thing?" A picture may be worth a thousand words, but it certainly is not a substitute for them.

First responders must be mindful of the fact that there may be many other people who work on a case who don't have the opportunity to attend the crime scene and see for themselves the appearance of the scene and the placement of the physical evidence within the scene. Detectives, attorneys and attorneys' investigators, and crime laboratory analysts all need to have an understanding of the origin of the physical evidence found at the scene, the appearance and condition of the evidence, and its relationship to the rest of the scene and other physical evidence within the scene. Describing the scene and the evidence in notes and reports, thoroughly photographing it, and providing sketches and diagrams provide the complete picture.

It is important that undisturbed areas at a crime scene are documented as well. Although it is important to thoroughly document the point of entry, and locations where the suspect may have moved through a scene and moved or removed items, it is equally important to document what was undisturbed. At a residential burglary scene where the suspect only stole jewelry from the master bedroom dresser, it is important to document undisturbed areas, such as the entertainment center, the sterling silver, or any other area containing valuables. This may reveal a great deal about the modus operandi of the suspect.

Photography

Photographing a crime scene may seem like a simple and commonsense task. But there are specific techniques that must be employed for a crime scene to be photographed correctly and thoroughly. By simply walking through a scene and taking snapshot photographs of items of evidence within the scene, the photographer may be missing important views or perspectives, and not giving the viewer of the photographs a complete visual record of the scene.

The first responder should begin with overall pictures of the scene. If the scene is a house or business, take photographs of it from the street and include the business sign or street address. Having photographs of the address makes it perfectly clear to the viewer where the photographs were taken. Include in these overall photographs the position of any vehicles in the area or the absence of any vehicles. It is also advisable for the photographer to turn his or her back to the scene and photograph the surrounding area. This will show pictorially the position or lack of other homes, structures, businesses, vehicles or overhead lights such as streetlights or parking lot security lights.

The photographer should continue taking overall photographs of the scene from various angles. When photographing a structure it is suggested to take photographs of it from all sides to get complete overall views of its entirety. When photographing a vehicle it is recommended that it is photographed from eight angles: the two sides, front, rear, and the four corners.

When completed with overall photographs, the first responder may move in and begin to take midrange, location-establishing photographs. These photographs will depict areas of interest within the scene, such as points of entry and egress, locations of missing property or property of value that is still there, and items of evidence within the scene. These photographs depict the locations of these areas of interest, establish their locations within the scene, and give a sense of their spatial relationship to other items of evidence within the scene. For example, if there is a beer can on a tabletop that has been identified as evidence, a midrange photograph would be a photograph showing the entire tabletop, giving the viewer a good sense of where the beer can is on the tabletop and its spatial relationship to everything else on the tabletop.

When the midrange, location-establishing photographs have all been taken, the first responder may then move in closer to take close-up photographs of areas of interest and items of evidence. These photographs are not to be confused with examination-quality photographs, which will be discussed in Chapter 6. Close-up photographs are simply photographs of the specific item or area as close as possible, depicting the detail of the item. In the previously mentioned example of the beer can on the tabletop, after the midrange photograph is taken, the photographer would move in and get close to the beer can and take a close-up photograph.

Thorough overall, midrange, and close-up photographs are necessary to provide a complete pictorial presentation of the scene and items of evidence within the scene. The photographs should depict the surroundings of the scene. They should also depict the undisturbed areas as previously described.

Video

First responders may not often have the opportunity to record a video of a crime scene, but a video can be a great investigative aid. A video may provide more of a three-dimensional representation of a crime scene. It can be used to demonstrate shot trajectories. It serves well to give a video or virtual tour of the scene. It can depict a scene more graphically.[*] And video may be best suited for demonstrating the view of a scene from the perspective of a witness, victim, or suspect.

If video is being used to document a scene from a witness's perspective, the photographer should stand where the witness stood and video record

---

[*] Barry A. J. Fisher, *Techniques of Crime Scene Investigation*, 5th ed. (Boca Raton, FL: CRC Press, 1993), Chapter 5.

the scene thoroughly by slowly panning 360 degrees. The video should cover every angle of the scene from the witness's perspective. If the witness moved through the scene and his or her perspective changed, the video should follow in his or her footsteps, again showing the witness's perspective of the incident.

In documenting an automobile accident the photographer can follow the approach to the point of impact, showing the driver's perspective prior to impact. The video should show any traffic control devices such as stop-ahead signs, stop signs, traffic lights, curve-warning signs, speed limit signs, and so forth. Any traffic control devices that may be obscured due to overgrowth of vegetation, damage, or any other reason should be documented in the video.

When video recording a scene it is recommended that the scene be recorded in one take, without repeatedly stopping and starting the tape. Stopping and starting can give the recording an edited appearance, which may be undesirable when presenting the tape in court. If the scene is the interior of a structure, stand back from each corner of the structure and slowly pan side to side to record the exterior of the structure from that angle, pause the recording and move to the next corner. Repeat this for all four corners. Then, once inside the structure, video record the scene without pausing. Hold the camera steady, move slowly and pan slowly.

Sketching

In addition to photographs and video, a crime scene sketch can assist in illustrating the scene and evidence found within the scene. When a crime scene sketch is combined with the photographs and video, it can help provide a clear and complete picture of the scene. When presenting photographs of evidence in court, it is of great benefit to jurors if the officer can present the photograph of the evidence, then point to a diagram and show where that evidence was found within the scene. People often understand and retain things they learn graphically better than things they learn only orally.

Crime scene sketches can be very useful in providing a record of details or conditions that are not easily recorded by other means. Large areas can be easily illustrated. Paths taken by subjects or vehicles can be demonstrated on diagrams more easily than photographs. Diagrams can be used as an aid when interviewing subjects or witnesses.*

A crime scene sketch need not be a work of art. Crime scene sketches can be drawn freehand and are usually very rough in appearance (Figure 2.1).

---

* Fisher, Chapter 5.

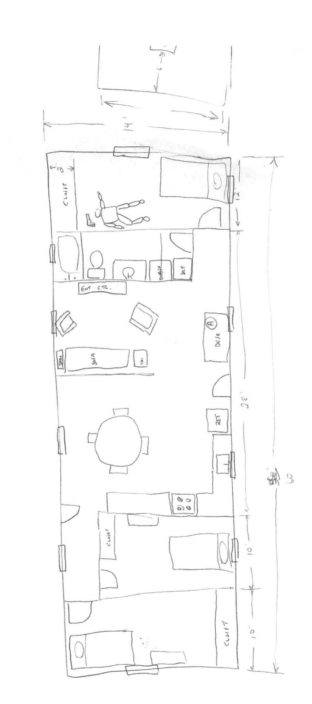

Figure 2.1 An example of a rough sketch done free hand at the crime scene. The rough sketch can later be recreated on a computer aided drawing program to create a more presentable illustration for investigators and court presentation.

A simple sketch depicting the scene, walls, fixtures, furniture, and evidence may be of great assistance to detectives, attorneys, and juries. Using different colored inks may assist the first responder in later interpreting the diagram. Black ink may be used for walls, fixtures, and furniture. Green ink may be used for dimension lines and legends. Red or blue ink may be used for different types of evidence. This may provide some clarity if the first responder doesn't see the diagram for several months or years and needs to review it for court or other purposes. It will be clear the green line is providing a dimension and not representing a wall or anything else.

Crime scene sketches need not be perfectly to scale. First responders are not expected to be great artists, architects, or engineers. While the sketch may lack in aesthetic value, it should still be an accurate representation of the scene.* The rough crime scene sketch may be preserved as evidence or a record. If the case eventually goes to trial, a final diagram may be produced from the sketch using a computer-aided drawing program and the assistance of someone familiar with how to use the program. The final diagram may be enlarged, mounted on poster board, and displayed in court on an easel, or saved in a digital format and projected onto a screen.

Courts have ruled that a crime scene diagram need not be perfect. In *Shook v. Pate* (50 Ala. 91) the court ruled "a diagram is simply an illustrative outline of a tract of land, or something else, capable of a linear projection, which is not intended to be perfectly correct and accurate." In *Deatria Doynell Hamilton v. State of Arkansas* the Arkansas Supreme Court ruled "a detective testified that the diagram was not to scale, but that it would assist the jury in understanding the location where various items were found … it simply identified locations at the crime scene and imported no implication of guilt."

Title box

A sketch should include a title box containing the essential information of the sketch. This should include the case number, the location of the incident, the date that the sketch was created, and the name of the person who created the sketch. The words "not to scale" may also be provided in the title box if the creator of the sketch chooses. A scale should not be provided on the rough sketch, as the rough sketch is drawn mostly or entirely freehand, and scale will not be accurately represented. If a scale is provided on the final diagram it should be presented graphically, not numerically (Figure 2.2). If a scale is provided numerically, for example, ¼″ = 1′, and the diagram is enlarged for investigative purposes or for presentation in court, then the scale will no longer be accurate, that is, ¼″ will no longer represent 1′.

---

* Gardner, Chapter 7.

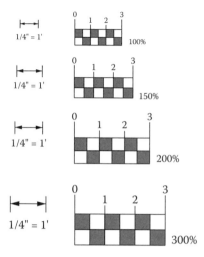

Figure 2.2 If a scale is provided it should be done graphically (right) rather than numerically (left).

Legend

A sketch should include a legend that provides essential information about the scene. It may be used to describe items within the scene and provide dimensions and measurements. By placing this information in a legend, rather than in the scene in the sketch, it can keep the diagram neat and clean. A sketch with measurements and dimension lines running to each item of evidence may become cluttered in appearance and difficult to interpret. The legend may be placed on the same paper as the sketch if there is room or placed on a separate sheet of paper.

Floor plan

There are different types of sketches that can be produced to show different perspectives of the crime scene. The most common type of sketch is a floor plan or overview. This type of sketch provides a bird's-eye view of the crime scene (Figure 2.3). From this type of sketch the viewer looks down into the scene and can understand the characteristics of the room or structure, the placement of furniture and fixtures, and the locations of evidence found within the crime scene. A floor plan sketch should provide an indication of direction. An arrow pointing north allows the viewer to correctly orient the diagram and understand directionality. Measurements of the overall room, structure, or scene should be taken, as should measurements to items of evidence within the scene.

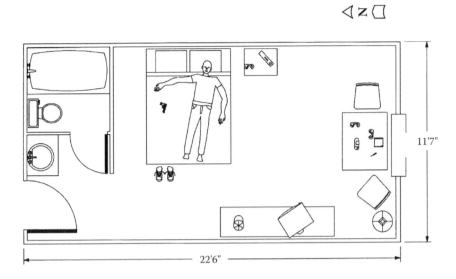

Figure 2.3 An example of a floor plan diagram.

Elevation diagram

An elevation diagram is a drawing of a vertical surface such as a wall or the side of a motor vehicle. This type of sketch is used when vertical surfaces contain evidence or anything related to the crime scene that needs to be documented. It is from the perspective of standing in the room and looking at the wall (Figure 2.4). The height and width of the wall or vehicle should be recorded as well as the height and distance from one edge to the evidence.

Exploded diagram

An exploded diagram is a combination of a floor plan sketch and an elevation diagram. It is as if a bomb detonates in a room and all of the walls fall straight out. In this type of sketch the viewer has a view of the complete floor plan and complete elevation diagrams of the entire room (Figure 2.5). It makes it very easy to visualize the evidence within the room and on the walls and easy to understand and tie together the spatial relationships of evidence within the room.

Perspective diagram

A perspective diagram is a three-dimensional view of the scene. These are generally very complex diagrams that may require more training and expertise than the first responder may have. A trained and experienced crime scene investigator may be able to produce a perspective diagram from the first

East wall elevation/impact mark

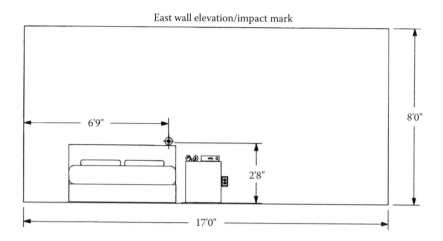

Figure 2.4 An example of an elevation diagram.

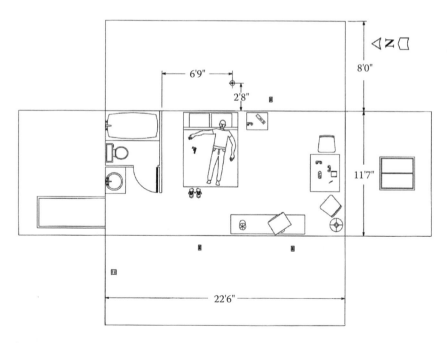

Figure 2.5 An example of an exploded diagram.

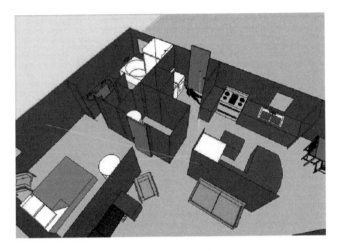

Figure 2.6 An example of a perspective diagram showing shot trajectories.

responder's sketch and notes. Perspective diagrams are well suited to show movement through a scene and shot trajectories (Figure 2.6). To create a perspective diagram, width, length, and height measurements need to be taken.

Methods of Measurement

Having size and dimensions measurements of the scene and evidence within is crucial for the scene to be reconstructed with some level of accuracy. There are many different techniques for taking measurements at a crime scene. Choosing the right method is based on the type of scene, whether indoor or outdoor, and the availability of fixed permanent objects to measure from. It is also a matter of habit and choosing the method that the first responder is most comfortable with and can use with the most efficiency.

When taking measurements it may only be necessary to round to the nearest inch or centimeter. Recording measurements to within fractions of an inch or millimeters may provide more detail than is necessary and only complicate the documentation of the crime scene and complicate the rough sketch. Recording measurements to within the nearest inch should provide sufficient accuracy for a final diagram to be produced, scene reconstruction, or courtroom presentation.

Choosing between measuring in English feet and inches and measuring in metric meters and centimeters depends on what is most common in the region in which the first responder works. In the United States, for example, juries may be most familiar with measurements in feet and inches and would understand spacial relationships in these measurements better than in metric measurements.

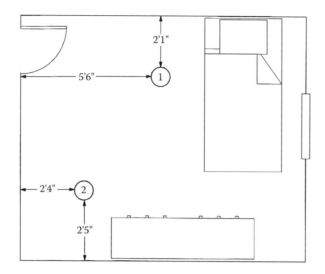

Figure 2.7 Rectangular coordinates are used in this scene to map items of evidence.

Rectangular coordinates

Perhaps the most common method of taking measurements at a crime scene is using rectangular coordinates. It is a simple method, used when a scene has clear boundaries such as interior walls. A measurement taken from the west wall and a measurement taken from the north wall will provide the rectangular coordinates (Figure 2.7).

If an object is large or odd shaped, multiple measurements can be taken to more accurately map its location. For example, if measuring a body, distances can be recorded to the approximate center of the head, the center of the abdomen or belly button, the right hand, the left hand, the right foot, and the left foot. Even more precise measurements could be taken to each hip and joint if desired.

Triangulation

The method known as triangulation as it is more commonly used may be more accurately referred to as *trilateration*. Using this method, the first responder measures from two fixed objects in the scene to the evidence to obtain the object's position. A fixed object should be something permanent such as a telephone pole, lamppost, or the corner of a structure (Figure 2.8).

Transecting baseline

The transecting baseline method is most commonly used for mapping outdoor scenes but can be used indoors. A baseline is established by laying out

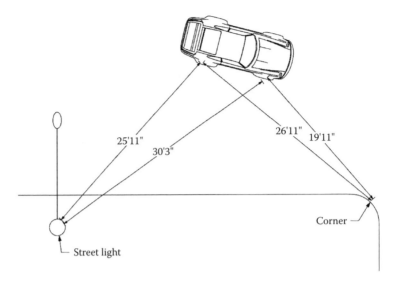

Figure 2.8 Triangulation was used by measuring from the light pole and the apex of the curved curb to the axles of the vehicle.

a tape measure between two fixed objects within the scene. The 0″ point on the tape measure becomes the baseline's datum point, or reference point. Measurements are taken at right angles from the baseline to each item and where that right angle intersects on the baseline. So the distance from the datum point to the intersecting right angle is recorded, and the distance from the baseline to the item is recorded (Figure 2.9).

A baseline could also be established along a straight fixed structure such as a fence line or wall. The datum point would be established at one end or corner. Measurements are then taken at right angles to the item, recording the distance from the baseline to the item, and the distance to the intersecting right angle from the datum point.

Azimuth or polar coordinates

This is an effective method for mapping evidence that may be scattered over a large open area with no fixed reference points. Areas like open fields, prairies, or meadows with no nearby trees, telephone poles, or other fixed objects are easily mapped using the azimuth technique.

Azimuth is the horizontal angle and distance from a fixed reference point to an object. A datum point, or reference point, is selected by finding the approximate center of the scene. That point is fixed using a global positioning system (GPS). A flat board marked with a circle and marked with 360 degrees is placed at this datum point, and the 0 degree mark is oriented to magnetic north (Figure 2.10). From that point, using a tape measure, record the angle

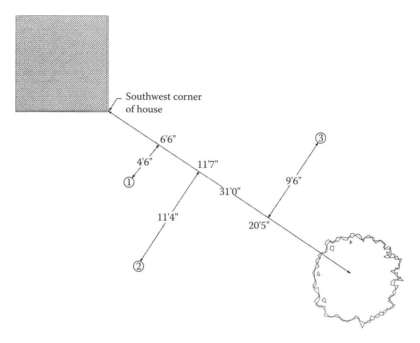

Figure 2.9 A transecting baseline was established from the corner of the house to the trunk of the tree.

and distance to each object (Figure 2.11). This method requires two people, one to hold the tape measure at the datum point and note the angle, and one to hold the tape measure at the object and determine the distance.

Commercial lasers or sighting devices are also available that can aid in this technique. The device is placed at the datum point and the user points the sighting device or laser at a sighting rod, which is held at the location of the evidence by an assistant. The device provides the angle and a tape measure is used to provide the horizontal distance measurement.

Notes and Reports

Note taking is a critical part of crime scene documentation. It is important for two key reasons. It forces first responders to commit their observations to writing. It enables them to keep a detailed record of everything they see and do. It is not infrequent to find some seemingly insignificant detail in an officer's notes become a key in the investigation at some later time.*

An officer's notes should include basic details such as the date and time the crime was reported, the date and time the officer arrived on scene,

* Fisher, Chapter 5.

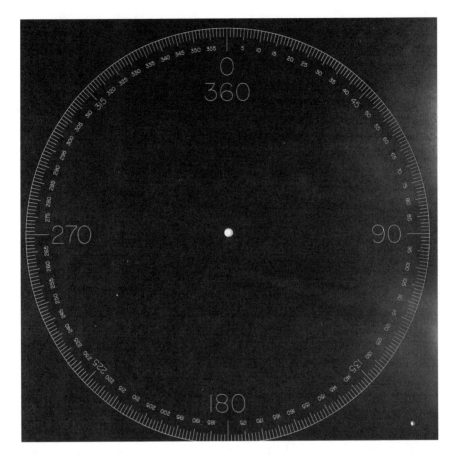

Figure 2.10 An azimuth board used to map evidence at the scene.

all persons present at the scene, the date and time the officer entered the scene, the date and time evidence was collected from the scene, and the date and time the officer cleared the scene. Notes should include all details of the officer's observations, including climate conditions, scents, and sounds. If the scene is indoors, included in the officer's notes should be whether lights are on or off and windows and doors are open or closed and locked or unlocked. Observations should be noted regarding any machinery or electronics in the house that are on or off. It should be noted if any heaters, fans, or air conditioners are running. Are there any televisions on and what channels are they tuned to? Are there any radios or stereos on and what station are they tuned to, or what type of music or program is playing?

Also included in the officer's notes should be negative observations. For example, if the point of entry into the crime scene is a window and the ground below the window is landscaping gravel and no footwear impressions

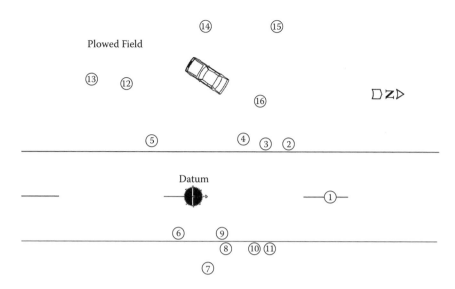

Figure 2.11 The azimuth board was used to map this scene when there were no fixed reference points from which to measure.

are found, this should be noted. If an area is thoroughly searched and no evidence is found, it should be noted that the area was searched and no evidence was found. Items may be processed for latent prints and none may be found. It is important for the officer to note what items were processed and the results, otherwise it may appear that this processing was not completed. Noting that these actions were performed not only shows the actions of the officer at the crime scene, it may prevent another investigator from returning to the scene to perform the same actions. As is often stated: "If it's not in a report, it never happened."

Also noted should be undisturbed areas. If a burglar enters the bedroom of a home and steals a female resident's panties but leaves behind valuables such as jewelry or electronics, this should be noted. Observing and noting items that are not disturbed or stolen may tell a great deal about the motives or modus operandi of the suspect.

Collecting Evidence

Once the scene has been searched, all evidence identified, note taking is completed, and everything is thoroughly documented, evidence may be collected and packaged. It is important that evidence is collected and packaged properly to preserve the evidence and prevent contamination. Once evidence is contaminated or damaged there is no way to turn back the clock and return it to its original condition.

When handling evidence that may have been handled by the suspect, it is important to handle it with clean latex or nitrile gloves, and gloves should be changed frequently. Try to handle the evidence in locations where the suspect may have not handled it in order to preserve latent fingerprints, trace evidence, or DNA.

Different packaging materials may be used depending on the type of evidence, as will be discussed in future chapters. But most types of evidence should be packaged individually in paper, cardboard, or some other type of breathable material. Plastic packaging should rarely, if ever, be used. Items that are trapped inside plastic with any moisture may mildew and mold. This can be very damaging to the evidence, and some types of evidence such as DNA may be completely consumed or destroyed by the mold and mildew. Whenever there is any doubt as to what type of packing to use, use paper.

Process for Latent Prints

Processing for latent print impressions, which will be discussed in detail in Chapter 9, is generally the last step in crime scene processing, as it is the most destructive step in crime scene investigation. When processing for latent prints it may become necessary to pick up items and move them around within the scene or remove them from the scene. When fingerprint powder and brush are applied to a surface, other evidence such as hairs and fibers may be lost or destroyed.

Anyone who has experience with fingerprint powder also knows how messy it can be. The fine powders used can be damaging to sensitive electronics and are very difficult to clean off of most any type of surface. A spilled jar of fingerprint powder in a victim's home can make them even more of a victim.

In some major cases or serious person's crimes it may be necessary to process the entire scene for latent prints. When processing property crime scenes for fingerprints, the first responder should concentrate on the points of entry and egress and items handled by the suspect. When processing vehicles, concentrate on the smooth surfaces such as painted exteriors, chrome, windows, mirrors, and seat belt buckles.

As with all techniques in crime scene investigation the first responder must use common sense and good judgment when using fingerprint powders. The risk of damaging property is very real and should be avoided if possible.

Chain of Custody

Chain of custody is the complete transmittal of evidence from its finding point at the crime scene to its submission in court. Every step of the chain of custody must be thoroughly documented to track everyone who has handled the evidence throughout its history. This may include the crime victim, the first responder, investigators, crime laboratories, attorneys, outside experts, and the courts.

Chain of custody begins when evidence is picked up from a crime scene. The first link in the chain of custody may be the first responder who collects the evidence, it may be the crime victim who picks up the evidence and hands it to the officer, it may be a nurse at a hospital collecting evidence from a sexual assault, or it may be anyone who first collects the evidence. Upon initial collection of evidence, the date and time should be noted. If first responders are handed evidence from someone else they should note the date, time, location, and condition of the evidence, then note what they did with the evidence, such as the date, time, and evidence locker they placed it in.

It is best to keep the chain of custody as short as possible. The adage is true that a chain is only as strong as its weakest link. If a first responder collects evidence at a crime scene, it is best that the same first responder submits it to the evidence unit at the agency. The author has personal experience with a case where a firearm used to murder two victims was first touched at the crime scene by a first responder who threw it away from the suspect while the suspect was being taken into custody. Another officer then picked up the firearm and secured it in the trunk of a patrol car. A detective then unloaded the firearm and secured it in a box. The box containing the firearm was then handed to the crime scene investigator who submitted it to the agency's evidence unit. All of these individuals handling the firearm were required to testify in court regarding from whom they received the firearm, the date and time they received it, and its condition. All of these extra links in the chain of custody made it more challenging to get the evidence admitted in court and could have resulted in the evidence being dismissed had an error been made.

Thorough documentation of the chain of custody and keeping unnecessary links out of the chain is essential for evidence to be admissible in a court of law.

Evidence

3

What Is Evidence?

Evidence can be defined as anything that sheds light on an incident or event. Virtually anything can be considered evidence. First responders will need to rely on their experience, training, and good judgment, in addition to what they know about the crime they are investigating, to determine what items at a crime scene are relevant to the incident and what items are not. If every item at a crime scene were considered evidence and collected, evidence storage locations would rapidly fill up and swamp crime laboratories with unmanageable backlogs. The first responders processing the crime scene are the filters who determine what items at the scene are relevant and should be considered evidence.

Direct Evidence

Some evidence is testimonial. Evidence gathered from the statements of victims, witnesses, and suspects is testimonial evidence, also known as direct evidence. It is evidence that establishes proof of a fact without any other evidence.* Another example of direct evidence may be a clear surveillance video showing the face of a robbery suspect.

Indirect Evidence

Physical evidence may be considered indirect evidence, also referred to as circumstantial evidence. It is evidence that can be seen, touched, smelled, or heard. Inferences may be drawn from it, but additional evidence may be necessary to prove a crime was committed and who committed the crime. For example, a subject's fingerprint may be found on a knife used in a stabbing but that does not mean that they are the person who committed the crime. It simply means that at some point in the history of that knife that person

---

* Wayne W. Bennett and Kären M. Hess, *Criminal Investigation,* 7th ed. (Belmont, CA: Thomson Wadsworth, 2004).

touched it. Additional physical evidence or testimonial evidence may be necessary to prove who stabbed the victim.

Class Characteristics

Some physical evidence may only be placed in a certain class, meaning it cannot be identified to a specific source. It may be possible to determine the make and model of a shoe or tire that made an impression at a crime scene, but it may not be possible to identify the mark at the crime scene to a specific individual shoe or tire. Carpet fibers collected from a crime scene may correspond to carpet fibers from the carpet in a suspect's vehicle in class characteristics, but they would also correspond in class characteristics to the carpet fibers in any other vehicle with the same type of carpet.

Although evidence that only displays class characteristics may not be identified to a specific source, it is still valuable evidence. And when presented in conjunction with other physical evidence or testimonial evidence, it may provide enough confirmation to develop probable cause or proof beyond a reasonable doubt.

Individual Characteristics

Some physical evidence may have unique characteristics that allow it to be identified to a specific source. Evidence such as fingerprints, DNA, and fired bullets contains unique details that can be used to identify it to one source to

Figure 3.1a Individual characteristics on the outsole of a shoe.

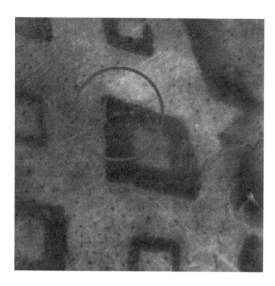

Figure 3.1b An impression made by the same shoe. The individual characteristics pointed out on the shoe outsole are observable in the crime scene impression.

the exclusion of all others. Shoes or tires that have accidental characteristics such as nicks, cuts, and gouges that occur randomly as they make contact with rough surfaces (Figure 3.1a), may also be identified to a specific source if those accidental characteristics are observable in the shoes or tires and are reproduced in the crime scene impression (Figure 3.1b).

Biological Evidence

4

Scene Safety

Processing crime scenes where biological evidence is present presents unique challenges to the first responder. As with any crime scene, first responders must primarily be concerned with their safety and the safety of others at the scene, and a scene with potential biological hazards can make this responsibility more challenging. Although the odds of contracting an airborne or bloodborne pathogen at a crime scene may be statistically low, the chances do exist, and can be reduced if the first responder follows some simple safety precautions.

There are four common routes of exposure to pathogens at a crime scene:

- Inhalation
- Ingestion
- Absorption
- Injection

Inhalation

Some pathogens a first responder may be exposed to may be present in the air. Flu viruses and tuberculosis (TB) can be transmitted when someone with the flu or active TB breaths out air that has the bacteria in it and another person breaths in the bacteria from the air. TB can cause damage to the lungs and other organs.[*] TB bacteria can survive even after the death of the infected person. There has even been a documented case of an embalmer contracting TB from a cadaver.[†]

A first responder at a crime scene who has a concern over possible TB infection should wear a face mask. Although it may not be practical to wear a mask at all crime scenes, the first responder should wear one in those cases where there may be a risk of exposure to TB bacteria.

---

[*] "Tuberculosis," Web MD, http://www.webmd.com/a-to-z-guides/tuberculosis (accessed June 20, 2009).
[†] "First Case of TB Transmission from Cadaver to Embalmer," Web MD, http://www.webmd.com/news/20000126/first-case-tb-transmission-cadaver-embalmer (accessed June 20, 2009).

Ingestion

Some pathogens can also be present in blood and other bodily fluids. Diseases such as human immunodeficiency virus (HIV), hepatitis B, and hepatitis C can be contracted through the contact of bodily fluids. Naturally a first responder would never intentionally ingest anything at a crime scene that may potentially contain a biological hazard. But it can happen inadvertently and precautions need to be taken to ensure that it does not.

First responders must avoid putting anything in their mouth at a crime scene. People are sometimes in the habit of putting a pen or pencil in their mouth when they need to free a hand for some other purpose. This must be avoided and is naturally avoided when the first responder is wearing a mask. Avoid smoking, chewing gum or tobacco, and eating or drinking in the crime scene. If first responders processing the crime scene needs to take a break for any of those reasons they should exit the crime scene and remove their gloves and clean their hands before handling anything they intend to put in their mouth.

Absorption

While our skin acts as a good barrier to viruses and bacteria, they can be absorbed through contact with skin and mucous membranes. Viruses and bacteria can also be absorbed through small cuts and scratches that are often present on hands.

First responders should avoid touching their face while processing a crime scene. They should avoid rubbing their eyes and nose to prevent exposure and should always wear latex or nitrile gloves when handling any evidence contaminated with possible bodily fluids. If first responders need to do anything such as blow their nose or remove a contact lens, they should exit the crime scene, remove their gloves, and wash their hands first.

Injection

Any sharp object contaminated with bodily fluids must be treated with extreme caution. A poke from a needle or a scratch from a knife, razor blade, or piece of broken glass could lead to potential exposure.

First responders should never place their hands anywhere they cannot see. Always look under a car seat, between and under sofa cushions, on the top shelf in a cabinet, or anywhere before reaching into that space. If sharp objects containing biological material are collected, they must be packaged in a puncture-resistant container and marked as a sharp object and biological hazard as a warning to anyone who may need to handle or open that package.

Searching for Biological Evidence

The most obvious technique used in searching for biological evidence is to simply perform a visual search. Many biological stains may be apparent to the naked eye and require only a simple visual search. Blood contrasts well against many background surfaces and is often easily detected. On surfaces such as a dark stained wood or a dark red fabric, bloodstains may not contrast as well and may require some effort to detect.

Blood absorbs ultraviolet light. A bloodstain on dark surface may be more easily visualized when viewed under ultraviolet light through an orange barrier filter (Figure 4.1). The stain will appear darker than the background and can then be documented and collected. There are many commercially available small ultraviolet lights that can be kept in a camera kit or crime scene kit and are as easy to use as a flashlight.

Other biological fluids, such as urine, semen, saliva, and vaginal secretions, may be very difficult to find on almost any surface. On white bed sheets these fluid stains may be very difficult if not impossible to see with the naked eye. However, these types of stains do fluoresce when viewed under ultraviolet light and become very easy to identify, document, and collect (Figure 4.2). The first responder may not be able to differentiate between stains of different biological fluid. For example, a saliva stain may look very much like a semen stain. All the first responder will know is that there is a stain present and must document and collect it properly. The determination of just what body fluid it is will need to be made at the crime lab.

There are many chemical enhancement techniques that can be used to search for or enhance bloodstains. These chemicals are generally not readily available to the first responder and are typically used only by trained and experienced crime scene investigators and forensic laboratory personnel.

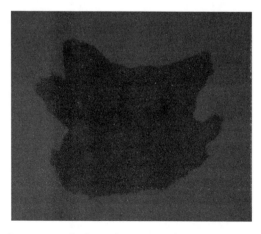

Figure 4.1 Bloodstain on a dark surface viewed under ultraviolet light.

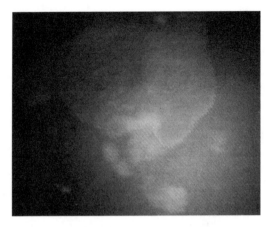

Figure 4.2 Semen stain viewed under ultraviolet light.

Documentation

Observations of the evidence must be included in notes and reports. There are many specific things that may be noted about a biological fluid stain. Record the date and time the stain is observed. Note the physical state of the stain (i.e., is it fluid, dried, and are there pools?), number of stains, and size of stains (measure). Are there shapes observed in the stains, such as drops or smears? Are the stains round or oblong? Are there patterns in the stains such as shoe prints, tire tracks, or fingerprints? (See Figure 4.3.) What are the atmospheric conditions? The temperature and humidity may have an effect on the condition of the stains. If the scene is indoors, note the temperature on the thermostat.

Stains should be photographed thoroughly using overall, midrange, and close-up techniques. They should be photographed without a scale to show them in their original state and photographed again with a scale to give the viewer some sense of how large the stains are or for life-size reproduction.

Biological fluid stains must be included in crime scene sketches or diagrams. Their position in the scene should be measured, as should their size and shape.

Collection

Whenever it is possible or practical, it is recommended to collect the item which the biological fluid stain is on. If the first responder has documented a bloodstain on a brick wall, it obviously is not practical in most cases to cut out the section of the brick wall and collect it. These stains may be collected

Figure 4.3 A fingerprint in blood.

through the use of swabs. But if the evidence is a beer can that may contain a suspect's saliva, it is practical to simply collect the beer can.

With some evidence the most practical thing to do may be to cut out the stain. For example, if the first responder investigating a crime scene detects a stain on a mattress, it is not practical in most cases to collect the entire mattress. A simple alternative is to cut out the fabric from the mattress that contains the stain.

If the item collected has a wet fluid stain on it, such as a wet bloody shirt collected from an assault victim, it is necessary to completely air-dry the item prior to packaging. Moisture trapped in the fabric can cause mildew, which can degrade and destroy DNA. The first responder should transport the item to the agency and secure it in a designated air-dry facility prior to packaging it, following the agency's procedures.

If the surface or object the stain is on cannot be collected or is not practical to collect, the stain may be collected using sterile cotton swabs. If the stain is fluid, a swab may be placed directly onto or into it to absorb the fluid (Figure 4.4). The swab must be allowed to air-dry and then packaged in paper according to department procedures. If the stain is dry, the swab may be moistened lightly with distilled water and then applied over the stain to collect the dried fluid. The swab should then be air-dried and packaged in paper.

When collecting biological evidence with swabs, it is often necessary to also swab the substrate or surface the stain is on. This is known as a surface

Figure 4.4 Swabbing a bloodstain from a surface.

Figure 4.5 Swabbing a surface control sample.

or substrate control sample. For example, if a bloodstain is present on a door handle, it is possible that the door handle may have contained other biological material, such as skin cells, from other people who have previously touched it (Figure 4.5). These cells, which contain DNA, may mix with cells from the bloodstain, which also contain DNA. When DNA analysis is performed on the swab of the bloodstain at the forensic laboratory, the result may be a mixed DNA profile. By swabbing the portion of the door handle that does not contain the bloodstain, a DNA analyst may be able to eliminate the stain from the background and individualize the DNA from the bloodstain. Surface control swabs are collected by lightly moistening the swabs and applying them to the surface next to the stain. They are then air-dried and packaged in paper.

For the same reason it is also necessary whenever distilled water is used to submit a control sample of the distilled water. Simply moisten a swab with the distilled water used to collect the stain, allow it to air-dry, and package it in paper.

Biological evidence must always be packaged in paper. Even though swabs are allowed to air-dry prior to packaging, they may still contain some moisture. As mentioned earlier moisture can lead to mildew, which may degrade or destroy DNA. By packaging biological evidence in paper it is allowed to breath and this may prevent mildew. If wet items are collected it may be necessary to temporarily package them in plastic to safely transport them to a facility where they can be properly air-dried before finally packaging them in paper.

Heat may also contribute to the degradation and destruction of DNA. When collecting biological evidence it is best to avoid storing it in the trunk of a patrol car on a hot day. It should be kept in the air-conditioned passenger compartment of a patrol car during transport from the scene to the agency's evidence storage facilities. Biological evidence is safest in cold temperatures and freezing will not harm DNA; in fact, it will preserve it.

Trace DNA

Some biological evidence is latent in nature, meaning it cannot be seen. Every day, people are shedding millions of skin cells. These skin cells are sometimes left behind on surfaces that we come into contact with and can be collected.

A man who was burglarizing rural homes in the area the author works in took his crimes a step further one day by murdering an elderly woman who lived in a home he intended to burglarize. It was believed that his modus operandi was to ring the doorbell of his victims' homes. If there was no answer he would force entry into the homes and burglarize them. In this case it was believed he rang the doorbell and the elderly woman answered. He killed her and stole property from the home. The doorbell was swabbed and a DNA profile was developed that matched the suspect. The crime was solved by hard-working detectives who traced the trail of stolen property back to the suspect. But the DNA profile from the doorbell placed him at the scene.

When attempting to collect trace DNA the first responder must be creative but practical. It is only necessary to swab surfaces that are believed to have been in contact with the suspect. For example, a forced-open window frame, a doorknob, or a burglary tool may contain trace DNA from the suspect.

It is important, however, not to overlook the possible presence of fingerprints in an attempt to collect trace DNA. It may be best to first process the pried-open window for fingerprints. If none are developed or only fingerprint smudge marks are developed, which contain no friction ridge detail, then the window frame may be swabbed for trace DNA.

Surfaces that are sometimes difficult to develop fingerprints on, such as the steering wheel of a recovered stolen vehicle, may be better served to swab for trace DNA. In these cases it is not necessary to collect surface control swabs, as the entire surface can and should be swabbed for trace DNA.

If other biological evidence is present at a scene, such as a scene where a burglar cuts himself upon forcing entry into a home and drops blood at the scene, it may not be necessary to attempt to collect trace DNA. The blood left behind by the suspect should be more than sufficient to obtain a DNA profile.

General Collection Tips

Use two swabs per sample. When collecting biological evidence, the more the better. If samples have degraded, forensic laboratories will have a better chance of getting conclusive results with a larger sample. Also, some states have laws that require forensic laboratories to notify prosecutors and defense attorneys whenever an entire evidence sample is going to be consumed during analysis. The defense then may have the option of having an expert present in the forensic laboratory when that sample is consumed and tested. If there are two swabs per sample, the forensic laboratory may consume one swab and save the other swab for the defense or for other future testing.

When collecting more than one swab per evidence sample, the swabs may all be packaged together as they are all from the same evidence stain. Use only enough distilled water to lightly moisten the swab. If the swab is saturated with distilled water it will not absorb the evidence sample as well. Try to collect the entire stain and concentrate the stain to the tip of the swab. This will make it easier for the analyst in the forensic laboratory to extract the sample.

Once the evidence is packaged, it should be marked on the outside of the packaging as a biological hazard. This warns anyone in contact with the package that it may contain infectious materials and should be handled with the appropriate precautions. Adhesive biohazard labels may be available to some first responders for such an application. If labels are not available, boldly write "biohazard" on the package as a precaution to others.

Presumptive Tests

There are numerous tests commercially available to test stains to presumptively determine if stains are blood. Tests such as these may be of value when a first responder is confronted with a stain that may be of some unknown origin. For example, if there is a red stain in a trash dumpster, it may be helpful to know if the stain is blood or just some other liquid of a more innocent nature prior to launching an investigation. These presumptive tests can help the first responder avoid a great deal of evidence collection and investigation if the stains are determined on scene to be something other than blood. Trained crime scene investigators and forensic laboratories should be familiar with such tests and should be able to assist with their application.

There are also tests that can not only help determine if the substance tested is blood but also help presumptively determine if it is human blood. This may be of benefit in some situations where the first responder believes it is likely that a stain is blood but is uncertain if it is human blood. For example, a red stain that appears to be blood is found on a roadside. It may be animal blood from an unfortunate creature that was struck by a car, or it may be human blood from an incident more sinister in nature. These types of tests, used at the scene, can presumptively differentiate between human and animal blood in such a situation.

Sexual Assault Kits

Sexual assault kits are generally used by specially trained hospital nurses known as sexual assault nurse examiners (SANEs). These examinations are typically performed in a hospital emergency room. The nurse collects all of the victim's clothing and then follows a step-by-step procedure to collect physical evidence from the victim's body. The evidence collected is returned to the kit and the kit is sealed.

Once the examination is complete the nurse will generally hand the victim's clothing and the sexual assault examination kit to a law enforcement representative. After receiving it from the nurse, the law enforcement representative should ensure that all clothing items are air-dried if necessary and packaged separately. The sexual assault kit must remain sealed and stored in a cool dry place. Refrigeration of sexual assault kits is preferable.

Combined DNA Indexing System (CODIS)

The Combined DNA Indexing System, or CODIS, is a national database that combines a database population of known DNA profiles and a database of DNA crime scene samples of unknown origin. These two databases search against one another looking for matches. When a match is made between a known profile and a crime scene sample, the forensic laboratory notifies investigators who are required to collect a DNA sample from the subject, usually in the form of buccal swabs, whose DNA profile matches the DNA profile from the evidence sample from the crime scene. A DNA profile is

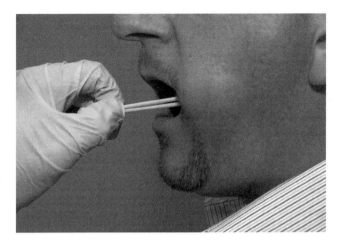

Figure 4.6 Buccal swabs being collected from a subject.

developed from the buccal swab of the subject and is then compared to the DNA profile developed from the evidence sample as a means of verifying the CODIS hit.

CODIS can also be helpful in solving cold crimes. DNA crime scene samples that are entered into CODIS today may not match any of the existing DNA profiles in the known offender catalog. However, the unknown DNA profile from the crime scene evidence stays in the system and will be searched against future known DNA profiles as they are entered into the system. This may result in hits on cold cases, which can result in the development of new suspects.

Elimination Samples

A practical and simple method for collecting DNA samples from known subjects is buccal swabs. Buccal swabs are swabs taken of the inside of the subject's mouth. Simply take two swabs in hand and swab the inside of the subject's left cheek, then with two additional swabs, swab the inside of the subject's right cheek (Figure 4.6). Allow all four swabs to air-dry and package them together in paper.

Elimination samples should be taken in cases where the victim's DNA could be mixed with the suspect's DNA. In cases such as assaults or sexual assaults where blood or other bodily fluids have been spilled and possibly mixed, elimination samples from the victim(s) should be taken for the forensic laboratory to eliminate the victim's DNA profile from the mixed sample. Also in cases such as a recovered stolen vehicle where trace DNA is collected from a steering wheel, the elimination sample from the owner of the vehicle may be helpful to the forensic laboratory to eliminate it from a mixed DNA profile.

Trace Evidence

5

Trace evidence can be found at virtually any type of crime scene. However, due to being trace in nature, it is easily overlooked. How many first responders processing a recovered stolen vehicle or the point of entry at a burglary scene regularly take the time or make the effort to search for and collect trace evidence? But the truth is, when the right techniques are applied, trace evidence can be very easy to search for and collect.

One of the easiest and most common methods for searching for and collecting trace evidence is using adhesive lint rollers. These are common and inexpensive household items that are excellent for collecting trace evidence. Simply apply the roller to the surface that evidence is being collected from to collect hair, fibers, or any other type of trace evidence mentioned later in this chapter (Figure 5.1). Once the trace evidence has been collected with the lint roller, the adhesive sheet is peeled off and packaged in plastic or paper. If the crime scene being processed is a car, one sheet of adhesive lint roller could be used for each seat and packaged separately.

When trace evidence is easily seen, such as a hair or clump of hair that was pulled in an assault case, or metal filings from a safe break-in, collection is as simple as picking up the evidence with a gloved hand or tweezers and packaging it in a paper bindle. Figure 5.2 is an example of a paper bindle, also known as a pharmacist's fold. When trace evidence is stored in this type of bindle it cannot fall out. Trace evidence such as hair packaged in a letter type of envelope could slip out through the seams in the envelope, causing it to be lost or no longer of value for analysis.

Another method of collecting trace evidence, which is very effective but not necessarily practical for the first responder, is the trace evidence vacuum (Figure 5.3). A specially designed filter is attached to the end of a vacuum hose and is used to collect trace evidence. The filter is removed from the vacuum hose, capped, and packaged. Although this is an effective method for the collection of trace evidence for crime scene investigators and forensic laboratories, it is impractical for first responders to carry a vacuum in their patrol cars, along with all of the other equipment they are expected to have with them on duty.

Figure 5.1 Trace evidence is collected with a common adhesive lint roller.

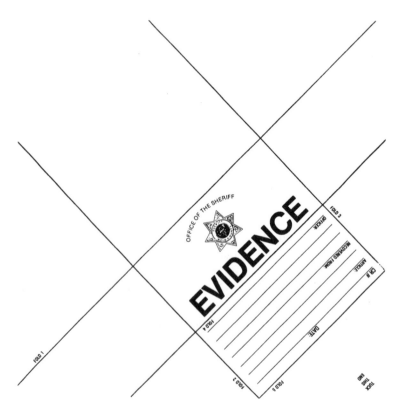

Figure 5.2 An example of a paper bindle.

Figure 5.3 Trace evidence vacuum filter.

Hair

Hair can be very valuable as trace evidence in many cases. A trace evidence analyst can glean a great deal of information from a single strand of hair. The species of animal can be determined through hair analysis. If the hair is human in origin a determination as to race or ethnicity may be made. It can be determined if the hair was cut, pulled, or naturally shed. The color and length of the hair can be determined. It can be determined if the hair has been dyed or bleached. It can even be determined from which part of the body the hair originated.

In addition to all of this, DNA can be extracted from hair and analysis can be performed to develop the DNA profile of the source of the hair. Hair shed at crime scenes should be collected and submitted to a forensic laboratory for all of these analyses (Figure 5.4).

If a DNA profile can be identified from hair, known exemplars from suspects, victims, and anyone else whom the hair and DNA profile should be compared to need to be collected. Collect known hair exemplars from a subject by pulling, not cutting. Collect at least twenty-five head hairs and collect them from five different locations on the head: the front (bangs), the top, the left side, the right side, and the back. This collection of head hair exemplars should be packaged together in a paper bindle.

If collecting pubic hair exemplars, they should also be collected by pulling, not cutting at least twenty-five hairs. They should be collected from different locations of the pubis and packaged together in a paper bindle.

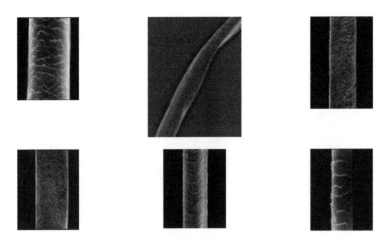

Figure 5.4 Scanning electron microscope images of human hair.

Fibers

Although fibers do not contain DNA and cannot be identified to a specific source, they can posses a variety of class characteristics that can be of great value to an investigation. There have been cases where the only physical evidence linking a suspect, victim, or crime scene is fiber evidence. A single carpet fiber or clothing fiber may seem insignificant, but if it connects a suspect to a victim or a crime scene it can be very powerful circumstantial evidence.

Fibers can be dyed in a variety of colors. Through analysis of fibers collected as evidence the color can be determined. It can be determined if the fiber is animal in origin, such as wool. It can be determined if the fiber is vegetable in nature, such as cotton, hemp, or flax. It can be determined if the fiber is mineral, such as fiberglass. And it can be determined if the fiber is synthetic, such as nylon or polyester. Synthetic fibers can also be made in a variety of shapes that can be examined by cross-sectioning the fiber (Figure 5.5). When a nylon fiber collected at a crime scene corresponds in color and shape, to a known sample fiber from a suspect's property this a powerful positive association.

Accelerants

Petroleum products such as gasoline and kerosene are sometimes used by arsonists to accelerate the spreading and progression of an intentionally set fire. Trained fire investigators attempt to locate burn patterns and fire points of origin, which may indicate the use of an accelerant at the fire scene.

  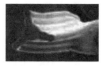

Figure 5.5 Scanning electron microscope images of cross-sections of nylon fiber. Synthetic fibers are made in a variety of shapes.

Samples of burned material can be collected from the fire's point of origin. These samples can be tested in a forensic laboratory to determine if there are any accelerants present. Samples of the burned material can be collected in quart- or gallon-size unused, unlined paint cans filled two-thirds to three-fourths full. A clean pair of latex or nitrile gloves should be used for each sample collected.

Paint cans are other pieces of equipment that may be impractical for first responders to carry with them. First responders may be reliant upon the fire investigator or crime scene investigators to have such evidence collection materials with them.

Wood

Wood may not often be considered as trace evidence, but in some cases it may be important, particularly in construction site burglaries where sawdust may be present. Remember in the Introduction we learned about Locard's exchange principle. If people walk through a site with sawdust on the floor they may remove sawdust from the site on their shoes, the cuffs of their pants, or even their shirt or coat if they pick up items from surfaces that contain sawdust.

A control sample of the sawdust may be collected from the scene and placed into a paper bindle. If a suspect is caught and sawdust is found on their clothing that matches the type of wood sawdust from the scene that coincidence may be very difficult to explain.

Soil

Soil may be thought of as any surface material, both natural and artificial, that lies on the earth's surface. Forensic examination of soil is not just concerned with the examination of naturally occurring rocks, minerals, vegetation, and animal matter; it also encompasses the detection of manufactured objects such as glass, paint chips, asphalt, brick fragments, and cinders, the presence of which may impart soil with characteristics that make it unique to a particular location. This material, when collected, may become very valuable physical evidence.*

When collecting control samples of soil from crime scenes, collect only the top surface layer that the suspect may have been in contact with. An amount equal to a tablespoon or two is sufficient. This may be packaged in a paper bindle, glass jar, or a plastic vial. Multiple samples may be collected from various locations at the crime scene and packaged separately. The location where each sample was collected should be noted.

If a suspect's clothing is collected with soil present, no attempt should be made to remove the soil from the clothing. Simply package each clothing item separately in paper with the soil intact.

Glass

Glass fragments collected from a crime scene may be very valuable evidence when compared to samples collected from a suspect. In the act of breaking a window there is a possibility that glass fragments may adhere to the suspect's clothing or hair. These fragments can be compared to control sample(s) collected at the scene. In cases of motor vehicle hit-and-run, broken glass fragments from the suspect's vehicle may be left behind at the scene. If collected, they can be compared to broken glass still remaining in the suspect's vehicle.

There are many different types of glass such as laminated glass; tempered glass; and soda-lime glass, which is used for normal window and bottle glass. These glasses can be manufactured with a variety of materials such as sand; soda (Na_2CO_3); lime (CaO); silicon oxides; and metal oxides such as aluminum, sodium, calcium, and magnesium.

Glass samples may be collected from a crime scene by placing them in a paper bindle. If there are multiple sources of broken glass, such as a broken window on a home and a broken window on a vehicle, these should be collected as separate samples. The suspect's clothing should be packaged separately in paper.

Plant Material and Seeds

Plant material can be removed from a crime scene in the same manner as any other type of trace evidence. Seeds may cling to a suspect's shoes or clothing. Grasses, weeds, and shrubs may cling to the undercarriage of a motor

---

* E. P. Junger, "Assessing the Unique Characteristics of Close-Proximity Soil Samples: Just How Useful Is Soil Evidence?" *Journal of Forensic Sciences* 41 (1996): 27.

vehicle. When a suspect walks or drives an area where plant material may be present (other than a common lawn), a control sample of plant material should be collected and packaged in paper. If a suspect's clothing is found to contain plant material, do not attempt to remove the plant material from the clothing. Simply package each clothing item separately in paper.

An example from the author's personal experience is a sexual assault case. A young girl was walking home from school on a rural road. A vehicle approached and stopped. A male exited the car and forced the young girl into the ditch where he sexually assaulted her. The suspect drove off and the girl walked home and reported the assault. Officers investigating the case found stickers commonly referred to as "goat heads" on the victim's back and clothing. The road was searched and a patch of this same plant material was found. The area where the patch of goat heads was found was searched and other evidence of the sexual assault was found.

Metals

Metals may be involved as evidence in a case where a suspect may have used a metal tool to force open a door or window, drill into or cut open a safe, or even grind off serials numbers from stolen property. Metal fragments may be present at the scene, and they may remain on the tools used in the act and on the suspect's clothes. If metal fragments are found at a crime scene they should be collected and placed into a paper bindle (Figure 5.6). If a suspect is developed and tools are found that may have been used during the commission of the crime, trace elements of the metals may be compared to determine

Figure 5.6 Metal fragments found at the scene of a safe burglary. This should be packaged in a paper bindle and preserved for comparison to metal fragments from tools suspected to have been used in the crime.

if they possibly came from the same source. Package the tools in a manner that will protect the working edge of the tool and preserve trace evidence, such as wrapping it in butcher paper.

Paint

In cases of vandalism where a victim's property has been spray painted (tagged) or in cases of motor vehicle hit-and-run, paint may become very important evidence. It can be analyzed for its chemical makeup and even layers of paint from motor vehicles can be compared. We understand that when two items come into contact there is an exchange of material from one to the other. When two vehicles collide the paint from the suspect's car may transfer onto the victim's car, and paint from the victim's car may transfer onto the suspect's car.

Collect these samples of paint by scraping the paint from the surface into a paper bindle using a clean razor blade. Scrape an area equal to about the size of a quarter, and scrape down to the metal surface.

Impression Evidence

6

Impression evidence at crime scenes can be very easily overlooked. Law enforcement officers, medics, firefighters, and witnesses don't always think about the potential for impression evidence to be present at a scene and therefore often track over impression evidence or fail to search for it altogether.

In his book *Footwear, the Missed Evidence*, Dwayne Hilderbrand states that footwear evidence is often overlooked because "the evidence is undervalued or misunderstood."[*] In some cases when footwear or tire impression evidence is documented at a crime scene, and is compared to a suspect's shoes or tires, there is only an association of class characteristics. The crime scene impressions may lack sufficient quality and quantity of detail to compare the unique accidental characteristics on the outsole of the shoe or the tread of the tire to the impressions. In such a case it may be the opinion of the examiner that the suspect's shoe or tire could have made the crime scene impression, but so could any other shoe or tire of the same physical size and design. This evidence can be viewed as very circumstantial. The general thought is if any shoe of the same physical size and outsole design could have made the impression, then it really does not place the suspect at the scene. Although this may be true, the odds of any other person in the general region of the crime scene wearing shoes of the exact same physical size, outsole design, and general wear are most likely very slim.

In his book *Footwear Impression Evidence Detection, Recovery and Examination*, William Bodziak writes, "The combined size and design characteristics of the shoes alone ... are so numerous and diverse when diluted among the approximately 1.5 billion shoes sold annually in the U.S., that any specific size and design of shoe, without regard to wear or other characteristics, will be owned by only a very small fraction of 1% of the general population."[†]

There are different types of impression evidence that may be categorized differently. Impressions may be latent (invisible) or patent (visible). Impressions may be two-dimensional or three-dimensional. Depending on the type of impression there is a variety of search techniques, documentation

---

[*] Dwayne S. Hilderbrand, *Footwear, the Missed Evidence* (Temecula, CA: Staggs Publishing, 1999), x.

[†] William J. Bodziak, *Footwear Impression Evidence: Detection, Recovery and Examination*, 2nd ed. (Boca Raton, FL: CRC Press, 2000), 4.

techniques, and collection techniques. With a little practice and experience, impression evidence can be easy to find, document, and collect at crime scenes, and can prove to be a very significant link between a suspect and the crime scene.

Two-Dimensional Impressions

Two-dimensional impressions, also known as contaminated prints, may be patent in origin (Figure 6.1). Impressions made in blood or grease may be very obvious and require little effort beyond a simple visual search. Two-dimensional impressions may also be latent in origin, meaning they require a little more effort to discover.

Two-dimensional impressions may also be wet in origin. An example of a wet-origin impression would be if one were to walk across a wet lawn, then enter a home and walk across a hard floor such as linoleum or hardwood. The moisture from the shoe will transfer to the floor, leaving a shoe impression. Two-dimensional impressions may also be dry in origin. If one were to

(a)   (b)

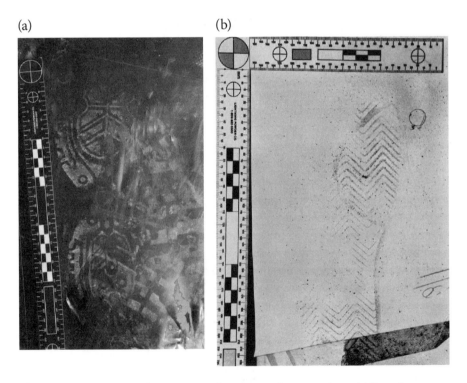

Figure 6.1 Examples of patent two-dimensional impressions. (a) Dust has transferred from a shoe onto black tile. (b) Automobile grease on a shoe has transferred onto a piece of paper.

walk across a dusty floor the dust may be removed from the floor onto the shoe, leaving a shoe impression. Or if one were to step onto a clean countertop, dust may transfer from the shoe to the countertop, leaving a shoe impression.

An effective technique to search for latent two-dimensional impressions is simply laying a bright flashlight on the surface to be searched and allow the light to skim across the surface. This search technique can be enhanced by dimming the lighting in the area to be searched, if possible. Impressions in dust can be observed using this technique, then documented and lifted. Figure 6.2 shows a tabletop that a burglar stood upon. In the ambient room lighting, no footwear impressions were observed. By dimming the room light and shining a flashlight across the table at a very low angle, a footwear impression was observed.

(a)

(b)

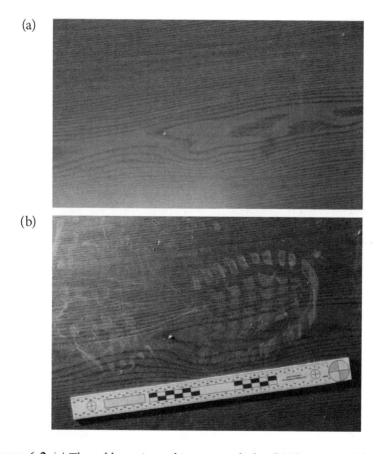

Figure 6.2 (a) The tabletop in ambient room light. (b) The same tabletop with very low oblique light. The footwear impression was almost invisible in ambient light but became very apparent when the room lights were dimmed and oblique light from a flashlight was shined across the tabletop.

Documenting Two-Dimensional Impressions

Impression evidence should be documented thoroughly in notes and reports. A simple crime scene sketch can be a useful visual aid to show locations of footwear evidence. A diagram may not only show where footwear impressions or tire impressions were located, it may also show the movement of a suspect through a scene.

Patent impressions should be photographed in place using the photographic techniques discussed in Chapter 2. Overall photographs depicting the entire scene, midrange photographs that establish the location of the evidence, and close-up photographs without a scale and with a scale can be used by examiners for comparison purposes. One photograph without a scale is taken to show the evidence in its natural state. Another photograph with a scale is taken, which can be used for 1:1, life-size reproduction.

It is recommended that the camera be placed on a tripod. This eliminates camera shake, which can result in blurry photographs. A small aperture should be used, such as f16 or f22. This allows for maximum depth of field for sharp focus. The photographer should fill the frame with the impression, which means getting as close to the impression as possible without cropping off the edges of the impression.

Photographing dust impressions poses more of a challenge. With the camera mounted on a tripod the photographer should use an off-camera flash with a synch cord to illuminate the impression. The camera flash held at a very low angle will create very shallow shadows within the impression to reveal the impression's detail in the photograph. A way to determine at which angle is best to hold the camera flash is to first hold a flashlight at various angles to determine at which angle the impression is best visualized. Then hold the camera flash in the same position while photographing. As with patent impressions, use a small aperture, fill the frame, and photograph the impression without a scale and with a scale. See Figure 6.2.

Collecting Two-Dimensional Impressions

Collecting two-dimensional impressions can be done with basic and simple materials, which the first responder can easily carry in a crime scene kit.

Whenever possible or practical it is best to collect the item the evidence is on. If a footwear or tire impression is apparent on a piece of cardboard, paper, lumber, or something else easily collected, collect the item and package it in a manner that will protect the impression, such as taping it or strapping it down into a gun box.

Wet-origin impressions are easily developed using traditional fingerprint powder. Once developed, they are photographed and lifted using standard fingerprint lifting techniques, which will be discussed in Chapter 9. Figure 6.3 is an example of a wet-origin impression on a linoleum floor, which was visible, but enhanced with fingerprint powder, photographed, and lifted.

Dry-origin impressions, impressions in dust, can be collected by using a variety of techniques. The techniques found by the author to be most practical are gelatin lifters and electrostatic dust lifters. Gelatin lifters are a fabric-backed lifter with a gelatin coating. These are available in white or black. When lifting a dust impression, a black gelatin lifter may yield the best result. A protective clear acetate is peeled off the gelatin lifter; the lifter is then placed onto the dust impression. Air bubbles can be reduced by applying the lifter to one end of the impression and laying it smoothly over the impression using a

(a)

(b)

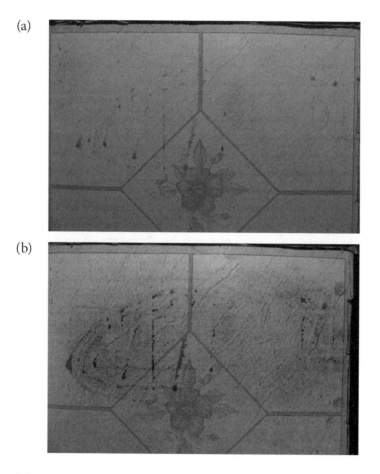

Figure 6.3 (a) A wet-origin impression on a linoleum floor. (b) The impression was enhanced fingerprint powder and lifted with fingerprint lifting tape.

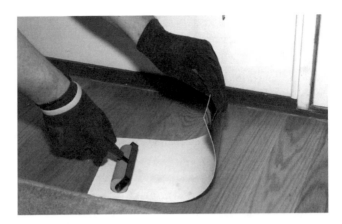

Figure 6.4 A gelatin lifter is used to lift a dust impression. A clean ink roller is used to apply the gelatin lifter, which will reduce or eliminate air bubbles in the lift.

roller such as a clean ink roller (Figure 6.4). The lifter is lifted off the surface and the clear acetate is applied using the roller to reduce air bubbles. This lifter can then be packaged in paper or plastic for final packaging.

Electrostatic dust lifters use a metalized film and an electrostatic charge to lift the dust impression using static electricity. The black side of the film is laid carefully over the impression. A grounding plate is placed next to the lifting film. The power supply unit is then placed on top of the grounding plate and the lifting film and turned on. This creates a static electric charge, which lifts the dust impression off the surface and onto the film. The film is placed into a manila folder, which will protect the fragile dust impression from disturbance. The folder can then be placed into a paper bag for final packaging. "Do not bend" should be noted on the packaging. Avoid storing the electrostatic dust lifting film directly in a paper bag or cardboard box. The film will continue to hold the electrostatic charge, and fibers from the paper or cardboard will cling to it. Electrostatic dust lifters may cause shock if not handled properly and should not be used on any conductive surface. The manufacturer's instructions should be followed to avoid injury.

Three-Dimensional Impressions

Three-dimensional impressions are impressions that are created when a hard object, such as a shoe or tire, is impressed into a softer object, such as soft soil, mud, or clay. Searching for these types of impressions often only requires a visual search. In darkness or in low lighting conditions, searching using a flashlight at an oblique (low) angle is most effective. Simply hold the flashlight low to the ground and let the light skim across the surface. This will create shadows in the three-dimensional impressions, making them more visible.

Documenting Three-Dimensional Impressions

Like two-dimensional impressions, three-dimensional impressions should be documented thoroughly in notes and reports and included in a crime scene sketch. They should also be photographed using the photographic techniques discussed in Chapter 2: overall photographs depicting the entire scene, midrange photographs that establish the location of the evidence, and close-up photographs.

Taking close-up examination-quality photographs of three-dimensional impressions is a little different from the techniques used to photograph two-dimensional impressions. Again the camera should be placed on a tripod, and the camera should be at a ninety degree angle to the impression. The frame should be filled with the impression, meaning that the camera should be as close to the impression as possible without cropping the edges of the impression.

One photograph should be taken without a scale to show the impression in its natural state and to show the condition of the surface immediately surrounding the impression. Then place a scale beside the impression. Never place the scale on top of or in the impression. The scale must be placed at the same depth as the bottom of the impression. The purpose of placing a scale in a photograph is so that the scale or size of the evidence in the photograph can be determined. A footwear examiner will use the scale in the photograph to reproduce the image to life size. If the impression in the photograph cannot be reproduced to life size, then the examiner will not be able to compare the physical size of a shoe to the physical size of the impression, thus severely limiting the results of the comparison. If the scale is not placed on the same plane or at the same depth as the impression, the impression cannot be reproduced to life size.

Figure 6.5 is an image of three photographic scales viewed from a ninety degree angle. They are placed one half inch apart in elevation. The highest scale appears to be much larger than the bottom scale one inch below it. If the scale is on a higher plane than the impression, when attempting to reproduce the impression to life size for comparison purposes, the impression will appear much smaller than it actually was on scene.

Getting the scale on the same plane and at the same depth as the bottom of the impression may require carefully moving dirt, rocks, debris, or snow aside in order to place the scale. Be very careful when doing this so as to not push dirt or snow into the impression (Figure 6.6).

With the scale properly placed, take a series of photographs of the impression using an off-camera flash to create shadows within the impression. If the conditions are sunny it will be necessary to cast the impression

(a)

(b)

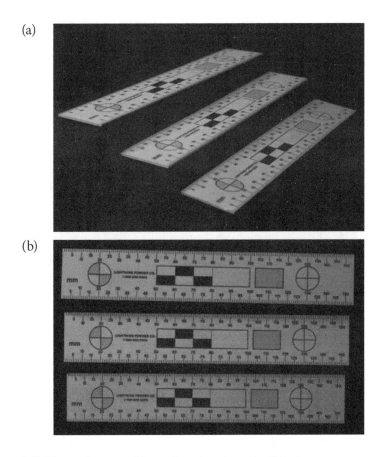

Figure 6.5 Three photographic scales placed one half inch apart appear much different in size when viewed from a ninety degree angle.

Figure 6.6 Snow or dirt must be pushed aside in order to get the scale on the same plane as the bottom of the impression.

in shadow. The off-camera flash must be the dominant light source in order to create shadows within the impression. Hold the flash in different positions around the impression to illuminate it from different directions and take three or four photographs. This will create different shadows within the impression, revealing different details. Details of the impression may be apparent with light coming from one direction, which may not be apparent with light coming from another direction. This is illustrated in Figure 6.7a and Figure 6.7b.

Figure 6.7a A photograph of a three-dimensional tire impression with the off-camera flash held at one angle.

Figure 6.7b The same impression with the off-camera flash held at a different angle, revealing different details within the impression. It is important to illuminate impressions from different directions to reveal the different details in the impression.

Choosing the Right Scale

There is much to know about selecting the right photographic scale. Using items such as business cards, coins, pens, or pencils are not appropriate substitutes for a proper photographic scale. Even items such as a tape measure or a ruler may not be appropriate for good examination-quality photographs. A good photographic scale is an essential item for any first responder's camera kit (Figure 6.8).

A good scale is flat. If a scale is curved or bent, different portions of the scale will be viewed at different planes or depths, and it will not be possible to reproduce that scale in an image to its actual size. A good scale has a matte or nonreflective surface. A glossy scale will reflect light and may have highlights where the details of the scale may be overexposed in a photograph. Scales should have features that allow for perspective correction if the photographer does not get the camera at a ninety degree angle to the impression. Small circles on the scale with intersecting lines within allow the crime lab to correct for any perspective off of ninety degrees. Good photographic scales also have thick black and white bars, which will still be able to be seen in an over- or underexposed image. The small marks on a scale, which indicate inches or centimeters, may not be visible in a poorly exposed photograph, but those heavier black and white bars should still be visible, allowing for accurate size reproduction of that image.

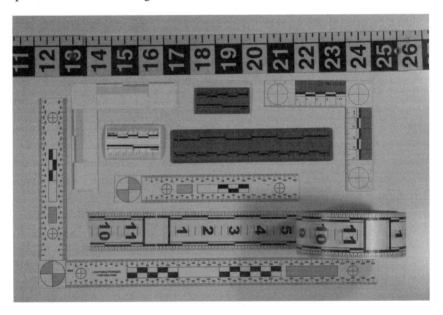

Figure 6.8 There are a variety of good photographic scales commercially available at low cost.

Casting Three-Dimensional Impressions

Casting impression evidence is a simple procedure involving inexpensive and easy-to-use materials. A casting of an impression has advantages over photographs to the examiner in the crime lab. The casting will generally render greater detail than photographs alone. The casting is a three-dimensional reproduction of the item (shoe, tire, tool, etc.) that made the impression. It is also a true-to-scale reproduction of the impression. If the scale in the photographs is not on the same plane as the impression, the photographs cannot be reproduced to life size, but the casting will always be a life-size reproduction of the impression. Photographing impression evidence is necessary, but scale, lighting, and focus can affect the quality of the photographs, whereas a cast is a more accurate and reliable reproduction of an impression.

The most common material used to cast impression evidence is a material called dental stone. Dental stone is a gypsum-based product much like plaster of paris. However, dental stone is easier to prepare and use, it sets up and cures quickly, and it has higher tensile strength than plaster of paris, meaning the casting is more durable and less likely to break after collection or lose detail when the dirt is cleaned off of it. Dental stone is available in bulk quantities, which can be divided into useable portions. It is also available commercially in premeasured and ready-to-use packaging. Water is simply added to the dental stone; it is mixed and poured directly into the impression.

When purchased in bulk, measure two pounds of dental stone into a one-gallon plastic ziplock baggie. When you are ready to make a casting of an impression, add ten ounces of water into the baggie and mix for approximately three minutes. The mixture should have the consistency of pancake batter or heavy cream. If the mixture is too thick simply add another ounce or two of water. If it is too thin add a little dry dental stone to the mixture.

Once the dental stone is mixed, it will begin to cure very quickly, so it is important not to mix for more than about four minutes. Once it begins to cure it will not easily pour and it may not completely fill in the impression. Begin pouring the mixture outside of the impression and let the mixture begin to run into the impression. Then quickly and smoothly pour the mixture into the impression. The result of this action is that the dental stone is not actually being poured directly into the impression, but dental stone is actually being poured into dental stone. Filling the impression with dental stone in this fashion should not damage the impression, but will preserve the detail of the impression. This is illustrated in Figure 6.9a and Figure 6.9b.

In most climactic conditions the dental stone casting may be picked up and collected after about thirty minutes. The cast is not completely

Figure 6.9a Begin pouring the dental stone outside of the impression, and then move across the impression, pouring dental stone into dental stone.

Figure 6.9b The resulting cast of a footwear impression.

cured at this point, however. It will take approximately twenty-four hours for the cast to cure. Do not attempt to clean dirt off the casting as this may result in damage or loss of detail. Simply package the casting in cardboard or paper with the dirt still clinging to it. Do not package the casting in plastic. It is still curing and will continue to give off moisture as it cures. It needs to be packaged in a breathable material so that this moisture can evaporate.

Casting impressions in snow poses more of a challenge. Dental stone is used to cast in snow also, but cannot be mixed and poured directly into the impression in snow. An impression in dry and granular snow can easily be disrupted or damaged by pouring in the dental stone. Dental stone also gives off heat as it cures, which can melt the impression.

A commercially available material known as "snow print wax," which is an aerosol spray wax, can be sprayed into the impression forming a waxlike shell into which dental stone can be poured. I have used this with mixed results. Another technique that I have found to be more successful is a method known as "dry casting" using a flour sifter and a pump spray bottle.[*] Sift a thin layer of dry dental stone into the impression. Then lightly mist the dry dental stone with cold water from the spray bottle. When the dental stone is moistened, sift in another light layer of dry dental stone, and moisten it with a mist of cold water from the spray bottle. Repeat this process until the impression is filled in with dental stone and allow it to cure for approximately thirty minutes. Then mix some dental stone in a plastic baggie and pour this mixture on top of the dental stone in the impression. This will act as reinforcement for the casting. Allow this to cure for another thirty minutes and collect the casting. The results of this technique may vary depending on the type of snow and the climactic conditions.

Tire Impressions, Special Considerations

Tire impressions are photographed and cast using the same techniques as footwear impressions. Overall and midrange photographs serve to establish the location of the tire tracks in the scene. Close-up photographs with scale and oblique light from an off-camera flash will reveal details within the impression.

It is necessary to attempt to document a complete rotation of the tire. If only a small two-foot segment of the tire impression is documented, accidental characteristics on the tire that were reproduced in the impression may not be documented in that two-foot section. Most passenger- and light-truck tires are approximately six feet in circumference. Taking close-up photographs of six feet of a tire impression will require that the impression be photographed in segments. Photograph a two-foot section, pick up the camera and tripod, move it over two feet, then photograph another two-foot section. Repeat the process for the third two-foot section. Overlap the two-foot segments slightly so that no portion of the impression is missed.

It is not practical to attempt to cast an entire six-foot segment of a tire impression. That would require a great deal of dental stone and would result in a very large and cumbersome casting, which would be very difficult to collect, package, and preserve. Casting a two- or three-foot segment is reasonable and more practical. Eight to ten pounds of dental stone can be mixed in a bucket and poured into the impression, resulting in a casting about two or three feet in length.

[*] Thomas W. Adair, "The Dry-Casting Method: A Reintroduction to a Simple Method for Casting Snow Impressions," *Journal of Forensic Identification* 57, no. 6 (2007), 823–831.

Figure 6.10 A vehicle in the scene turned and left impressions of all four tires.

If there are two tire impressions side by side from the driver's side tires and the passenger side tires of the suspect vehicle, it may be possible to measure the stance of the vehicle that made the impressions. Vehicle stance is the width of the axle from one tire to the other. For example, a pickup truck will obviously have a wider stance than a compact car. Determining the stance of the vehicle may provide an investigative aid.

To measure the stance of the vehicle, simply measure from the outside edge of one tire impression to the inside edge of the other. This will give you the approximate stance of the vehicle. It is not necessary to measure the width of the individual tire impression; a study has shown that the width of an impression made by a tire can vary greatly depending on the amount of air pressure in the tire and the weight of the cargo in the vehicle.*

In some cases only the tracks of the rear tires are present. The rear tires track over the front tires when the vehicle is moving forward. When a vehicle backs up or makes a turn in the crime scene, impressions of all four tires may be present and should be documented (Figure 6.10).

Tool Marks

Tools, like shoes or tires, can have both class and individual characteristics. A screwdriver may be the same physical size and shape as every other screwdriver manufactured in the same way (class characteristics), but as

---

* Jan LeMay, Thomas W. Adair, Angela Fisher, Jennifer James, and Brittany Boltman, "Air Pressure and Cargo Weight Affect the Width of Tire Impressions," *Journal of Forensic Identification* 58, no. 6 (2008), 660–665.

that screwdriver is used the edge will acquire random unique characteristics (individual characteristics). The tool may impart those characteristics on a surface or material that it is applied to.

Tools can leave marks in two different ways. A tool mark impression is when the tool is impressed into a softer surface, such as when a pry bar is applied to a door to force it open (Figure 6.11a). A striation is when the tool is dragged across a surface, leaving scratch marks.

Tool marks are photographed and documented the same way as footwear and tire impression evidence. Casting tool marks may also be performed with dental stone if dental stone is all that is available. However, there are many polymer-type casting products commercially available that may perform better than dental stone when casting tool marks. Many of these products involve simply mixing a pliable plastic material with a catalyst. This mixture is pressed into the tool mark and allowed to harden. The results are often castings of tool marks that reproduce microscopic detail of the impression (Figure 6.11b).

Databases and Other Investigative Aids

A footwear or tire track examiner may be able to review the photographs and castings of impression evidence from the crime scene and be able to determine which make and model made a specific impression. The examiner has access to various databases, books and publications, Web-based searches, and a network of other footwear and tire track examiners. Determining the make and model of a shoe or tire can assist the investigation greatly. For example, if a string of burglaries is occurring in a specific geographical

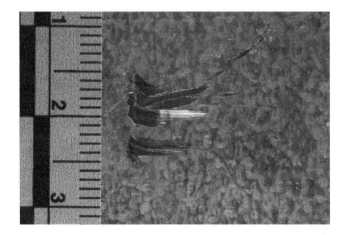

Figure 6.11a A tool impression on metal.

Figure 6.11b A Durocast® casting of the tool mark.

area, and one common connection between the crime scenes is an impression made by a specific make and model of tire, officers and investigators can canvass the area, looking for vehicles with those specific make and model tires. If footwear impressions are recovered from a burglary scene, a footwear examiner may be able to determine the make and model of the shoes that made the impression. Then, when officers or investigators are searching a suspect's home, they only need to seize the shoes of that make and model.

When searching for a specific make and model shoe, do not stop when one pair is found. Often people will have multiple pairs of the same-style shoe. Search until all like pairs are found. Also include in the search receipts and shoe boxes. Tires have warranties and people may keep the receipt as proof of purchase. They may then dispose of the tires and may forget to dispose of the receipt. Shoe boxes are often kept in homes for use as storage containers. In one case, a footwear examiner was able to determine that impressions left at a crime scene were made by Nike Air Force 1 shoes. A search of the suspect's home was conducted and no Nike Air Force 1 shoes were found, but a shoe box for the same make and model shoes was found, suggesting that the suspect had owned a pair of the shoes.

Firearms Evidence 7

Safety

First responders have a great deal of responsibility at a crime scene, not the least of which is scene safety. They are responsible for the safety of themselves, victims, witnesses, bystanders, emergency medical personnel, other officers, and even suspects. This responsibility can be amplified when firearms or other dangerous weapons are present at the crime scene. This may mean that in some circumstances a firearm may need to be moved to a safe location before medical personnel can enter a scene to render aid to a victim. If this is the case, the first responder who takes responsibility for moving that weapon will be responsible for documenting its location and condition prior to being moved. This may require some simple notes, a rough sketch, and a few quick photographs before picking up and moving the firearm. For this reason, it is recommended that all first responders keep a camera available to take photographs at a moment's notice. Keep the camera's disposable batteries fresh or rechargeable batteries charged. Keep the camera loaded with film or a memory card. This way, if photographs are required, the camera is ready to go simply by turning it on. Take an overall, midrange, and close-up photograph of the firearm and note its condition. The firearm may then be removed from the scene and its location and condition will have been adequately documented.

If a crime scene can be secured without moving the firearm, this is preferable. Move all subjects at the scene to a safe location outside the perimeter of the crime scene. A search of the scene may be necessary to ensure there are no additional subjects remaining within the scene, such as suspects or additional victims or witnesses. Once the scene is deemed safe and it has been secured, there should be no need for the firearms to be moved or removed from the scene. Leaving the firearm in its original location and original condition will be of the most benefit to detectives, crime scene investigators, and coroners or medical examiners who may be responding to assist with the incident.

If the responsibility of documenting and collecting the firearm falls on the first responder, then proper firearm safety rules must be applied. Safety rules that the first responder learns on the shooting range apply at the crime scene as well. Always assume the firearm is loaded, always keep the muzzle pointed in a safe direction, and never touch the trigger. It is not unheard of for accidents to happen with firearms at crime scenes, which have resulted in property damage, injury, and even death.

Understanding Firearms

Law enforcement officers generally have a good understanding of how firearms operate. They receive this training and knowledge from firearms instruction and practice on the shooting range. It is important, however, to also understand how the functions of firearms affect spent bullets and shell casings, and what investigative value these effects offer. There is a great deal of information that firearms experts in forensic laboratories can glean from firearms evidence recovered from the crime scene.

When the trigger is pulled on a firearm the firing pin impacts the primer, causing the primer, which is a small shock-sensitive explosive round, to detonate. This ignites the gunpowder, which burns very rapidly, creating gases that rapidly expand inside the cartridge casing. The rapid expansion of these gases creates force that pushes the cartridge casing back against the breach face of the firearm and propels the bullet rapidly down the barrel (Figure 7.1). All of this applied mechanical force will leave markings on the casings and bullet that will be unique to the firearm, and allow the casing and bullet to be compared and identified to the firearm from which they were fired.

Caliber

Firearms are manufactured in a variety of different calibers. Caliber is the measure of the bore of the barrel. It is measured in either millimeters,

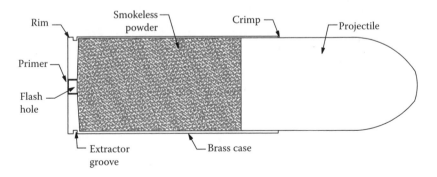

Figure 7.1 A cartridge consists of a primer, casing, gunpowder, and projectile or bullet.

Figure 7.2 A 9-mm firearm has a bore width of 9 mm.

hundredths of an inch, or thousandths of an inch. For example, a 9-mm fire-arm has a barrel with a bore width of 9 millimeters (Figure 7.2). A .45 caliber firearm has a bore width of 45 one-hundredths of an inch. A .243 caliber firearm has a bore width of 243 one-thousandths of an inch.

Rifling

Handguns and rifles use rifling, which forces the projectile to spin as it travels down the barrel and continue to spin as it travels through the air. Rifling is a system of spiraled raised and lowered portions of the barrel interior known as lands and grooves. As the bullet travels through the bar-rel this spiraling system causes the bullet to spin. It is this spinning action that allows the bullet to fly straight through the air rather than tumble and change direction. Rifling characteristics can be different from fire-arm to firearm. The number of lands and grooves can vary as well as the widths of lands and grooves, and the direction that the lands and grooves spiral down the barrel. Some barrels are made with a left-hand twist and some are made with a right-hand twist (Figure 7.3). These rifling charac-teristics are impressed on the bullet as it travels down the barrel and are class characteristics that may be helpful in the firearm's examination. A firearms examiner can analyze these class characteristics and determine the number of lands and grooves, the widths of the lands and grooves, and the direction of twist. This information may allow the firearms examiner to determine the make, model, and caliber of the firearm that fired the bullet.

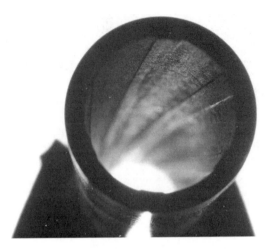

Figure 7.3 This photograph of a barrel bore reveals the rifling inside the barrel. This barrel has six lands and six grooves with a right-hand twist.

Individual Characteristics on Bullets

There can be unique tiny imperfections in the barrel of a firearm created at the time of manufacture or through use of the firearm. These imperfections may cause small scratches or striations on the bullet as it travels down the barrel of the firearm. These striations will be unique to the firearm that fired the bullet (Figure 7.4). A firearms examiner will test fire the firearm and compare the test-fire bullet to the bullet recovered from the crime scene in a comparison microscope. The two bullets are viewed side by side and the unique striations are compared. It may be possible to determine that the two bullets were fired from the same firearm or conclude that they were not fired from the same firearm.

Shell Casings

The most obvious thing to note about spent shell casings at a crime scene is the head stamp. This is the marking stamped by the ammunition manufacture into the base of the casing. This may reveal information about the caliber of the firearm that fired the shots and the manufacturer of the ammunition (Figure 7.5).

When the gunpowder burns and the bullet is forced down the barrel, there is equal force pressing the casing against the breach face of the firearm. The breach face may contain unique characteristics as a result of the weapon manufacturing. These unique characteristics may be impressed onto

Figure 7.4 The small scratches or striations on a bullet are unique to the firearm that fired it. The jacket of this spent bullet reveals the rifling and the unique striations imparted on the bullet by the barrel of the gun.

Figure 7.5 The head stamp on this shell casing reads S & B 45 AUTO. The head stamp markings should be noted and reported.

the shell casing and may be compared to test-fired shell casings to determine whether the casings recovered from the crime scene and the test-fired casings were fired from the same firearm.

The firing pin, which strikes the primer, will have class characteristics such as its size and shape. This will be impressed into the primer and can be compared between test-fired casings and casings recovered from the crime scene. The firing pin may also possess unique imperfections resulting from the manufacturing process or from use, which can be compared.

The extractor pin is a device that extracts spent shell casings from the chamber of automatic or semiautomatic weapons. The extractor pin can also leave an impression on the shell casing, which can be compared to test-fired casings.

When searching for live ammunition it is important to collect all of the ammunition found in the search. The firearms examiner will want to use the same ammunition used in the shooting for the test fires and comparisons.

Shotguns, Shells, and Wadding

Shotguns, unlike handguns and rifles, do not have rifling. The bores of shotguns are typically smooth and do not impart any characteristics on the projectiles as they travel down the barrel. The bores of shotgun barrels are measured in gauges. The smaller the gauge, the larger the bore of the barrel. For example, a twelve-gauge shotgun has a larger diameter bore than a twenty gauge. Shotgun projectiles can range from a single large slug to dozens of small pellets. These projectiles are forced down the barrel of the shotgun by wadding. Wadding is packed into the shotgun cartridge between the gunpowder and the projectile(s) or shot. When the gunpowder burns, the gases push the wadding out of the cartridge casing and down the barrel, and the wadding pushes the shot. Upon exiting the barrel the wadding will fall off much faster than the shot, and the shot will continue downrange (see Figure 7.6a and Figure 7.6b). It is important to search for, document, and collect the wadding at crime scenes where a shotgun was involved. The wadding can provide information as to the gauge of the shotgun used, the size of the shot, and manufacturer of the ammunition.

National Integrated Ballistics Information Network (NIBIN)

The National Integrated Ballistics Information Network (NIBIN) is a database managed by the Federal Bureau of Investigation (FBI). It has satellite terminals in many state and local law enforcement agency forensic laboratories. It is a database that contains images of breach face impressions and

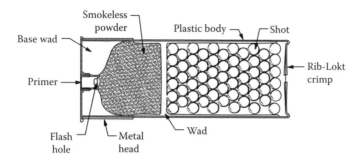

Figure 7.6a An illustration of a shotgun cartridge showing the different components.

Figure 7.6b A shotgun cartridge disassembled: the casing, gunpowder, wadding, and shot.

firing pin impressions on spent shell casings. The database searches these images against each other and attempts to find corresponding characteristics between them to determine if they were fired from the same firearm. The purpose of this is to attempt to connect crimes in which the same firearm may have been used.

Say one law enforcement agency has a shooting incident and shell casings are left behind by the shooter at the scene. A few weeks later another neighboring law enforcement agency has a shooting incident, and again shell casings are left behind by the shooter at the scene. If both of these agencies documented, collected, and submitted these shell casings to a forensic laboratory with access to the NIBIN system, NIBIN would find the corresponding characteristics of these shell casings and link the two crimes by the firearm used.

The NIBIN database can be used in another fashion. If a firearm is seized for any reason it can be sent to the forensic laboratory. It will be test fired, and images of the breach face impressions and firing pin impressions will be entered into NIBIN. The system will then search these test-fired casings against casings recovered from crime scenes in an attempt to determine if the seized firearm was used in any of those crimes.

NIBIN can be a great investigative tool when it is used. In cases where shell casings are documented and collected from a crime scene and there is no suspect or no weapon to compare the casings to, they should be submitted to the forensic laboratory for entry into NIBIN.

Many firearms manufacturers today are test firing their firearms before they are sent to retailers. They send a test-fired casing to the FBI along with information on the make, model, and serial number of the firearm. These test-fired casings are entered into NIBIN before the firearm is even sold. Casings from crime scenes may "hit" on one of these firearms in NIBIN and then the purchase records of the firearm can be investigated to assist in tracking the owner of the firearm.

Gunshot Residue

Gunshot residue consists of the microscopic particles that can be left behind on a shooter's hands and face when discharging a firearm. Barium and antimony are common elements used in ammunition, and particles of these elements are what are searched for in gunshot residue analysis. There is a variety of gunshot residue collection kits available commercially and from forensic laboratories. A law enforcement agency should consult with the forensic laboratory that will be performing the analysis to find out which collection method the laboratory prefers.

Gunshot residue is transitory and perishable. Subjects who are going to have a gunshot residue collection kit performed on them should not be allowed to wash their hands or place their hands in their pockets. The collection should be performed as soon as possible after the incident (Figure 7.7). If subjects are to be handcuffed and transported prior to gunshot residue collection, their hands should be placed in clean paper bags taped around the wrists to attempt to preserve the evidence.

There is some subjectivity to gunshot residue analysis. A person may test positive for gunshot residue, but this does not necessarily mean that he or she discharged a firearm. They may have simply been in the proximity of a firearm when it was discharged, or may have handled a firearm without discharging it and gunshot residue particles transferred onto them.

Locard's exchange principle applies to law enforcement officers, too. First responders handle and fire their duty weapons on a regular basis. They may carry multiple firearms in their vehicles and handle those firearms daily. Officers may have a handgun, rifle, and less-than-lethal firearm that they carry in their patrol vehicle every day. They routinely train with these

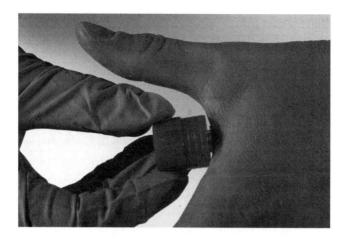

Figure 7.7 A gunshot residue collection kit is performed on a subject by dabbing the collection stubs on the subject's hands.

weapons, firing dozens or hundreds of rounds a year through each. It should be expected that law enforcement officers may at any time have gunshot residue particles on their hands and clothing. Gunshot residue particles may also be present in their patrol vehicles. For these reasons it is imperative that first responders wear clean latex or nitrile gloves before attempting to perform a gunshot residue collection kit on a subject, and perform that collection as soon as possible before the subject is handcuffed or transported in a patrol vehicle.

Handling, Unloading, and Packaging Firearm Evidence

Firearms may contain other pertinent evidence in addition to the ballistic evidence. Firearms may contain fingerprints, DNA, and trace evidence. The smooth, flat portions of the firearm are the most likely places to contain fingerprints. In a close contact or contact type of shooting it is possible that the firearm may have blood or tissue on it. Trace DNA may also be left behind on the firearm by the person who handled it. Firearms should be handled in a manner that will preserve this evidence. Handle firearms only with clean latex or nitrile gloves. Handle them by the rough textured portions of the grip.

There is a great variety of types of firearms, varying in their use and function. It is impossible for a first responder to be familiar with every type of firearm, their function, and operation. If faced with a unfamiliar firearm and unsure how to safely handle and unload it, contact an armor, range instructor, or anyone who may be able to unload the firearm safely before attempting to unload it yourself and possibly causing an accidental discharge or damaging the firearm.

Before unloading a revolver, use a marker to make a small mark on the cylinder beside the top strap of the revolver. This way, when the cylinder is opened, the chamber, which is in the top position in-line with the barrel, can be noted. Note and photograph the condition of the ammunition in each chamber. Note if there are spent casings or live cartridges and note the head stamp marking on each casing or cartridge. Photograph the cylinder, showing the condition of the ammunition loaded in the firearm (Figure 7.8). Also note if the chamber rotates to the right or to the left. Each cartridge or casing should be packaged separately.

When unloading a semiautomatic firearm, first remove the magazine from the firearm. The magazine may be unloaded or be left in its loaded condition and packaged separately. Lock back the slide to remove any ammunition that may be in the chamber. Any casings or cartridges in the chamber should be noted, photographed, and packaged separately.

Firearms should be packaged in a cardboard box or according to department policy. They should be packaged unloaded and in a safe condition. Nylon zip ties may be used to hold revolver chambers open or hold the slides back on semiautomatics. This way when the box is opened for examination the person opening the box can see that the firearm is unloaded and safe. Nylon ties may also be used to secure the gun in the

Figure 7.8 The cylinder of a revolver should be photographed and documented prior to being unloaded. Note the condition and position of ammunition in the cylinder.

Figure 7.9 A semiautomatic handgun packaged in a box. Nylon ties are used to secure the firearm in the box and to hold the slide open. When packaged in this fashion anyone opening the box can clearly see that there is no ammunition in the firearm and it is in a safe condition.

box, which will prevent it from sliding or moving around in it (Figure 7.9). If the firearm has blood or tissue on it, the box it is packaged in should be marked as a biohazard to warn anyone opening it to use universal precautions.

When handling or packaging a firearm one must never put anything in its barrel. Picking up a firearm by putting a pen or pencil in the barrel, or securing nylon ties in the barrel can alter the imperfections in the barrel, which make the unique striations on bullets fired through it. This could alter the appearance of test-fired bullets and alter the results of any forensic tests. Figure 7.10 is an example of a firearms unloading worksheet that is helpful in documenting the condition of the ammunition in the firearm upon unloading.

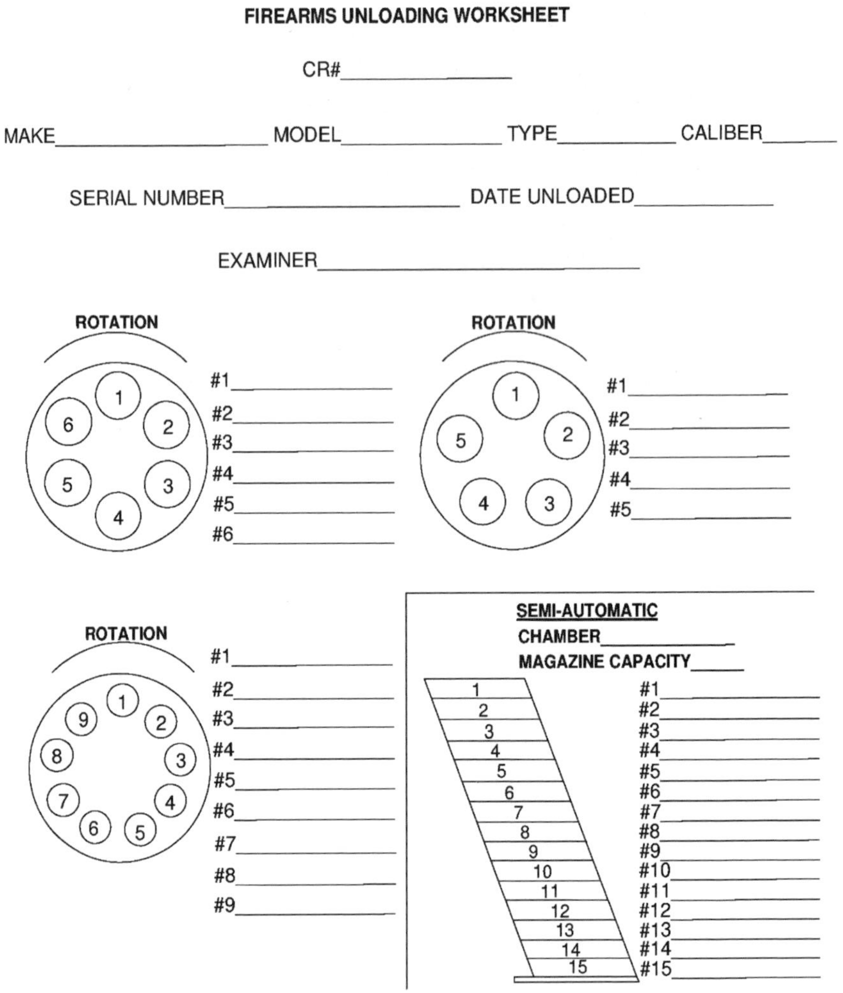

FIREARMS UNLOADING WORKSHEET

CR#_____

MAKE_____ MODEL_____ TYPE_____ CALIBER_____

SERIAL NUMBER_____ DATE UNLOADED_____

EXAMINER_____

ROTATION

1
6   2
5   3
4

#1_____
#2_____
#3_____
#4_____
#5_____
#6_____

ROTATION

1
5   2
4   3

#1_____
#2_____
#3_____
#4_____
#5_____

ROTATION

1
9   2
8   3
7   4
6   5

#1_____
#2_____
#3_____
#4_____
#5_____
#6_____
#7_____
#8_____
#9_____

SEMI-AUTOMATIC
CHAMBER_____
MAGAZINE CAPACITY_____

1
2
3
4
5
6
7
8
9
10
11
12
13
14
15

#1_____
#2_____
#3_____
#4_____
#5_____
#6_____
#7_____
#8_____
#9_____
#10_____
#11_____
#12_____
#13_____
#14_____
#15_____

Figure 7.10 An example of a firearms unloading worksheet.

Documents

8

Handwriting

Like fingerprints, no two people's handwriting is exactly alike. Experts in handwriting analysis can compare known samples of an individual's handwriting to unknown sources of handwriting, such as that on a forged check, credit card receipt, or threatening note, and determine if they came from the same source. Experts can also determine if a signature on a document is authentic, forged, or traced. When handwritten documents are found to be evidence in a case, they should be properly collected and preserved, and it should be considered whether handwriting analysis may be of benefit to the investigation.

Known samples of an individual's handwriting must be obtained for the purpose of comparison. There are two types of known sample standards that can be obtained. First, *informal standards* or *nonrequest samples* are those writings from the normal course of business. Things like checks, credit card receipts, handwritten notes, and employment records are excellent sources of known standards of an individual's handwriting. The second type of sample standards is *requested standards*, which are prepared by the subject at the request of an investigator. Obtaining these standards may require a court order if consent is not given and should be witnessed by the investigating officer. It is best to submit both informal standards and requested standards for comparison.

When obtaining requested standards choose white paper that is of similar quality to that which the questioned writing is on and have the subject use a similar writing instrument as was used to create the questioned writing. When the subject has completed one form, remove the form before he or she begins another. This will make it difficult for the subject to copy a writing style from one form to another.

Except for fill-in-the-blank forms, dictate the text to the subject. Duplicate the same letter combinations, phrases, and words as seen in the questioned writing without exactly duplicating the context of the questioned writing. Compose the text in advance so it is prepared prior to the meeting with the subject. Dictation of the text should take place at least three times, removing the handwriting sample after each dictation. This will make it difficult for the subject to disguise his or her handwriting.

Signature samples are best obtained when the subject is required to combine other writings with a signature rather than simply writing a set of signatures alone. Have the subject completely fill out twenty to thirty separate sample checks in different amounts, each of which will include a signature (Figure 8.1).*

The "London Business"† text may also be dictated to the subject several times, removing each sample upon completion. Have the subject complete other exemplars between dictations of this text:

> Our London business is good, but Vienna and Berlin are quiet. Mr. D. Lloyd has gone to Switzerland and I hope for good news. He will be there for a week at 1496 Zermott St. and then goes to Turin and Rome and will join Col. Parry and arrive at Athens, Greece, Nov. 27th or Dec. 2nd. Letters should be addressed: King James Blvd. 3580. We expect Chas. E. Fuller Tuesday. Dr. L. McQuad and Robt. Unger, Esq., left on the 'Y.X.' Express tonight.

In addition to the check handwriting exemplars, composed dictation, and the London Business text, other sample forms may be provided to the subject to obtain handwriting standards. Figures 8.2, 8.3a, and 8.3b are examples of handwriting exemplar forms that the subject may also complete. Mixing the forms, checks, and dictated text will make it difficult for the subject to disguise his or her handwriting consistently from one handwritten sample to another.

Typewriters

Although typewriters may be rare, there are still some in use today. Analysis of typewriters may be able to identify or eliminate a specific machine or a single element. It may be able to classify the questioned typewriting to a manufacturer and type style. It may be possible to examine the typewriter ribbon for the questioned text and possible physical match back to the questioned typewriting. And it may be able to date the questioned writing.‡

Whenever possible the typewriter should be submitted for examination. Collect all typewriter ribbons and elements in the vicinity of the typewriter. Look in drawers, on shelves, and in trash cans. Do not attempt to use the typewriter or change any of the existing settings.

---

* Richard Saferstein, *Criminalistics: An Introduction to Forensic Science*, 6th ed. (Upper Saddle River, NJ: Prentice Hall, 1998), Chapter 16.
† Albert S. Osborn, *Questioned Documents*, 2nd ed. (Chicago: Nelson-Hall, 1989).
‡ Colorado Bureau of Investigation, *Physical Evidence Handbook* (2007).

Sample checks filled out by _____,
this _____ day of _____ 19___, for the purpose of handwriting
comparison.

Witnessed by _____

GREELEY, COLORADO _____ 19____ No. _____

THE GREELEY NATIONAL BANK   82-120
                                                              1021

PAY TO THE
  ORDER OF _____ $ _____

_____DOLLARS

FOR _____

PLEASE WRITE
ACCOUNT   ▶ [   ]
NUMBER HERE   _____

  1:1021"'0120 1:

GREELEY, COLORADO _____ 19____ No. _____

THE GREELEY NATIONAL BANK   82-120
                                                              1021

PAY TO THE
  ORDER OF _____ $ _____

_____DOLLARS

FOR _____

PLEASE WRITE
ACCOUNT   ▶ [   ]
NUMBER HERE   _____

  1:1021"'0120 1:

GREELEY, COLORADO _____ 19____ No. _____

THE GREELEY NATIONAL BANK   82-120
                                                              1021

PAY TO THE
  ORDER OF _____ $ _____

_____DOLLARS

FOR _____

PLEASE WRITE
ACCOUNT   ▶ [   ]
NUMBER HERE   _____

  1:1021"'0120 1:

▲   PAYEE ENDORSEMENT AREA   ▲   ▲   PAYEE ENDORSEMENT AREA   ▲   ▲   PAYEE ENDORSEMENT AREA   ▲
▼ THIS AREA FOR BANK USE ONLY ▼   ▼ THIS AREA FOR BANK USE ONLY ▼   ▼ THIS AREA FOR BANK USE ONLY ▼

Figure 8.1 An example of a check handwriting exemplar.

PERSONAL INFORMATION FOR HANDWRITING EXEMPLAR

Full Name: _____

Address/Phone: _____

_____

Date & Place of Birth: _____

Highest education level achieved: _____

Occupation:_____   Current Employer: _____

Employer Address/Phone: _____

_____

1.   Are you currently taking any drugs or medications?_____

     What kind? _____   How often? _____

     Doctor/name? _____   Last time taken _____

2.   Are you currently under the influence of any drug, medication or alcohol? _____

     If so, explain _____

3.   Are you being/have you even been treated for any alcohol or drug related problem?____

     If so, explain _____

_____

4.   With which hand do you normally write? _____

5.   Can you write equally well with both hands? _____

6.   Have you suffered any injuries which may affect your present writing ability? _____

     If so, explain _____

_____

_____   _____
Witness   Date/Time   Signature   Date/Time

Figure 8.2 An example of a personal information form to be completed by the subject providing the handwriting exemplar.

				1. Case Number	

HANDWRITING EXEMPLAR
WRITE IN INK – DO NOT PRINT UNLESS TOLD TO DO SO – DO NOT ABBREVIATE

2. Name (First Middle, Last)					3. Race	4. Sex
5. Street Address		City	State	6. Telephone		
7. Place of Birth				8. Date of Birth		8a. Age
9. Color of Hair	10. Color of Eyes	11. Height	12. Weight		13a. ( ) Right Handed b. ( ) Left Handed c. ( ) Ambidextrous	
14. Present Employer				15. Occupation or Title		
16. Employer Address				17. Telephone		
18. List All Names and Nicknames You Have Used						
19. Nearest Living Relative				19a. Relationship		
19b. Address of Nearest Relative		City	State	19c. Telephone		
20. Name and Location of Last School Attended				21. Last Grade Completed		
22. Write Alphabet in Capital Letters						
23. Write Alphabet in Small Letters						
24. Write the Months of the Year						
25. Write the Days of the Week						
26. Write the Numerals 1 through 9, Repeat as space allows						
27. Write the Numbers in Longhand; One, Two, Three, etc., as Space Allows						
28. Write the Numbers in Longhand; Ten, Twenty, Thirty, Forty, etc., as Space Allows						
29. Write the Numbers in Longhand; One-Hundred, Two-Hundred, Three-Hundred, etc., as Space Allows						

Figure 8.3a Page one of two of a handwriting exemplar form.

Computer Printers

Analysis of computer printers may assist in identifying or eliminating a specific printer. It may also assist in classifying the type print to a printer type and possibly to a manufacturer.*

If a printer can be located it should be submitted for examination whenever possible. Note the condition of the printer and all other associated

* Ibid.

COPY ALL OF THE FOLLOWING MATERIAL IN LONGHAND		
30. a. Dr. Albert Barth	b. Mr. Charles G. David	c. King Soopers
d. Elliott L. Frank II	e. Mrs. George I. Harding	f. Safeway
g. Johnson & King Co.	h. Lewis Y. McNeale 3rd	i. Target
j. Odell Perez Sr.	k. Miss Queen Roberts	l. Albertson's
m. Thomas X. Smith Jr.	n. United Van & Storage	o. J. C. Penney
p. Wolff Z. Young	q. First Savings & Trust Co.	r. Westland
s. Jefferson Building	t. Missionville, Mississippi	u. Del Farm
v. Honolulu, Hawaii	w. Denver, Colorado	x. LaRelle's
y. Rocky Mountain	z. Lakewood, Colorado	aa. Zales Jewelry
bb. Montgomery Ward	cc. Sears, Roebuck & Co.	dd. Shopping Mall
ee. Hold on Now	ff. A glass	gg. Virginia
hh. Trouble	ii. dollars	jj. no cents
kk. In Luck	ll. shut up	mm. we jump
nn. Hard Cash	oo. speed demon	pp. by each one
qq. Title Year	rr. Bombs away	ss. Stickup
tt. Kill an Ibex	uu. Neusteter's	vv. Colfax and Wadsworth
ww. I'll Never See Him Again	xx. On Million Dollars in Cash	

| 31.

a. Witness_____

b. Witness_____

32. Date _____ Time _____ | 33. Right Index Print | 34. The above is a specimen of my handwriting which has been given voluntarily. They are accurate exemplars of my handwriting.

Signature_____

Date _____ Time _____ |

Figure 8.3b Page two of two of a handwriting exemplar form.

equipment, such as scanners and software. Do not attempt to use the printer or change any of the existing settings. If the printer cannot be submitted, then submit all questioned documents along with other printed documents within the vicinity of the computer equipment. These samples may have been generated from the printer in question.

Paper and Ink Analysis

Analysis of paper may establish a paper source or origin. It may be able to determine the authenticity and possible date of manufacture of the paper.

Figure 8.4 An example of a torn edge physical match.

It may assist in establishing if two samples of paper were derived from a common source. If the paper has a torn edge, such as a piece of notepaper torn from a pad, a comparison may be performed to determine if there is a physical match between the questioned document and a possible source (Figure 8.4).*

Ink may be analyzed to determine whether the ink from one entry on a document is consistent with other entries. An analysis may assist in determining if two ink formulations contain the same chemical dyes and may be able to eliminate a specific ink formulation.†

Indented Writing

Indented writing occurs when writing on the top sheet of paper on a pad is impressed or indented into the page beneath it. Document examiners may be able to decipher the indented writing. They may also be able to determine the origin of the writing on the questioned document, the sequence of pages, and if there were alterations or insertions to the questioned document. The first responder should collect any pads, blotters, sheets of paper, or any other substance that may have been indented by a writing instrument.‡

Collection and Preservation

Always wear clean disposable gloves or use tweezers when handling questioned items. Paper documents can be very good sources of fingerprints.

---

* Ibid.
† Ibid.
‡ Ibid.

Protect the documents for potential fingerprints and DNA when appropriate. Try to avoid folding documents. If folding the documents is necessary, only fold at preexisting creases.

Documents should be maintained in a cool, dry storage area. Do not expose documents to humidity, bright light, or unusual heat. Do not place them in the trunk of a car in the summertime. Package all questioned and known items separately. Write on the evidence packaging prior enclosing the evidence items to avoid adding indentations to the documents. Do not staple or paperclip the questioned documents. Clearly identify the documents to be examined for indented writing on all lab transmittal forms.

There are chemical processes that the forensic lab can use to develop fingerprints on paper. These methods may be preferred over attempting to process with fingerprint powder in the field and are performed after the document analysis has been completed. Do not attempt to process questioned documents for fingerprints in the field if they are to be submitted to the forensic lab.

Fingerprints

9

For over one century fingerprints have been used in criminal cases to place individuals at crime scenes or prove they had contact with an item of evidence. Fingerprints are circumstantial in nature. A fingerprint found on a firearm does not mean that the individual who deposited the print ever fired the weapon. It simply means that at some time in the history of that firearm that individual touched it. Despite its circumstantial nature, fingerprint evidence can be very compelling and can often lead to pleas of guilty or convictions at trial. Through database searches, fingerprint evidence can even provide an investigative lead in a case with absolutely no suspects.

Although the term used here is *fingerprints* it should be understood that when referring to fingerprints we are including within that term impressions of all friction ridge skin. Many friction ridge impressions recovered from crime scenes and off evidence are actually palm prints, and on rare occasions barefoot or toe impressions. Any friction ridge impression may be of value to an investigation, regardless of its friction ridge skin source.

Fingerprint identification has been used to complement other means of identification. Even identical twins, with identical DNA, do not have the same fingerprints. There have been documented cases where an identical twin could be identified as being present at a crime scene or in contact with evidence only through fingerprints. Conversely, there have been cases where DNA evidence has exonerated individuals who had previously been charged or convicted through erroneous fingerprint identifications. These cases illustrate the importance of documenting and collecting all physical evidence that is reasonable and relevant at a crime scene. If blood from a suspect is found at a crime scene that can be used for DNA analysis, that does not mean that it is no longer necessary to search for fingerprints, and vice versa.

A common public misconception is that fingerprints are often found at crime scenes because every time a person touches an object a fingerprint is left behind. In many cases, fingerprints that are of value for comparison purposes are not found. Fingerprints can be related to a rubber stamp. If a stamp is clean and dry, and pressed onto a surface, it will not leave an impression. The same is true of fingerprints. There must be some residue or matrix on the finger to transfer to the surface touched. If a rubber stamp is over inked, it will leave a large deposit of ink on the surface and the detail will be unclear. The same is true of fingerprints. If a person is perspiring heavily and the fingers are wet with sweat, he or she will deposit very wet impressions with unclear detail. If a rubber stamp is placed on a surface and dragged off, it will leave a smudged impression. This is also true of fingerprints. The finger must be placed down on the surface and lifted straight off to avoid smudging the impression. If a rubber stamp is applied to a textured surface the ink will transfer to the tops of the surface but not the depressed portions of the surface, leaving an incomplete impression. The same applies to fingerprints. If the surface is dusty or dirty, the dust will interfere with the transfer of the ink from a stamp to the surface. The same also applies to fingerprints. There are many conditions that can affect the clear deposition of fingerprint residue from friction ridge skin to a surface.

Patent Impressions

A patent impression is one that can be seen and requires no development. These may be impressions in blood, grease, oil, ink, paint, and so forth. These can be found with a simple visual search, and this search can be aided by a bright light source such as a flashlight. It is best to always photograph these impressions, as will be discussed later in this chapter. Attempting to enhance patent impressions with fingerprint powder and lifting them could damage the impression. After photographing a patent impression, it is best to collect the item the fingerprint is on whenever possible (Figure 9.1). Package it and transport it in a manner that will protect the impression from vibration or frictional forces; packaging in a plastic bag may cause the bag to be in contact with the impression and rub on it. If it is not practical to collect the item, the photographs may have to suffice.

Latent Impressions

The term *latent* has become synonymous with a crime scene fingerprint, but really refers to a print that cannot be seen or is difficult to see and will require some development. This is a fingerprint typically deposited in perspiration or oils from skin. A search for latent impressions can be aided by a bright flashlight held at a very oblique or low angle to the surface, allowing the light to skim across the surface (Figure 9.2). A search for latent impressions may also require applying fingerprint powder to the surface to develop impressions that cannot otherwise be seen.

Figure 9.1 A photograph of a patent impression in blood. If the item the finger-print is on cannot be collected, the photographs may be the only way to preserve the fingerprint.

Figure 9.2 A latent print photographed with oblique light from an off-camera flash.

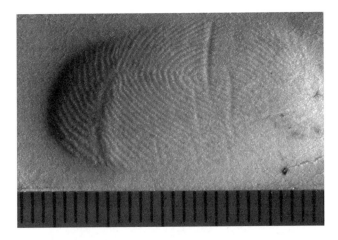

Figure 9.3 A plastic fingerprint impression in modeling clay. A plastic impression is a three-dimensional impression resulting when friction ridge skin is pressed into a soft object.

Plastic Impressions

Plastic, in this sense, means capable of being shaped or formed, that is, pliable.* A plastic impression is a three-dimensional impression resulting when friction ridge skin is pressed into a soft substrate such as clay, putty, butter, chocolate, or any other soft material (Figure 9.3). These impressions must be photographed using oblique light from an off-camera flash, as described in Chapter 6. After photographing, and whenever possible, the item the plastic impression is on should be collected and preserved. If the impression is on a material that could melt, like butter or chocolate, it should be preserved in a refrigerator.

Searching for Fingerprints

Searching for fingerprints most often is performed by simply applying the traditional fingerprint brush and powder to the surface being searched. In some cases, like the recovery of a stolen vehicle, it may not be practical or possible to search and process the entire vehicle with fingerprint powder. Fingerprint powder is also very messy and difficult to clean up. If the first responder gets carried away with fingerprint powder while searching for fingerprints, a huge mess could be created, making the crime victim even more of a victim than he or she already is. It is important when processing a scene or evidence with

---

* William Morris, ed., *The American Heritage Dictionary*, Second College Edition (Boston: Houghton Mifflin, 1982).

fingerprint powder to concentrate on areas that are known to have been or are likely to have been handled by the suspects. When processing evidence inside a home or office, carry the evidence outside when possible to process it. This will reduce the amount of fingerprint powder used inside and will minimize the mess left behind for the victim.

Developing and Lifting Fingerprints

There are a variety of materials which fingerprint brushes are made from. Some of the more common are fiberglass, camel hair, squirrel hair, and feathers (Figure 9.4). Which one is best comes down to the personal preference of the user. It is recommended that the first responder try a variety of different brushes to determine which gives the best results.

Hold the brush with a light grip and lightly dip the brush into the fingerprint powder. Tap off the excess powder from the brush. A common mistake made when using fingerprint powder is getting too much on the brush. Using too much powder may result in the entire fingerprint being filled in with powder, and the ridge detail can be lost. Gently apply the brush to the surface using only the tip of the brush (Figure 9.5). Do not brush with the sides of the brush, as this may smear or distort the delicate fingerprint residue. Distribute the powder evenly and smoothly.

Once a fingerprint has begun to develop it should be "dressed" by gently brushing away all of the excess powder. Brush in a direction that follows the ridge flow of the fingerprint and, again, use only the tip of the

Figure 9.4 Fingerprint brushes are made from a variety of materials, such as fiberglass, camel hair, and feathers.

Figure 9.5 Brush gently with the tip of the brush, not the sides of the brush.

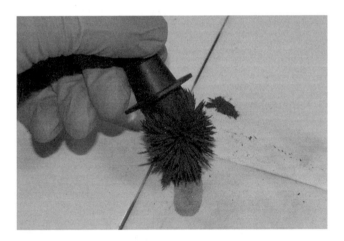

Figure 9.6 A magnetic brush and powder are applied to a surface. The only thing in contact with the impression is the powder itself, reducing or even eliminating the chance of distorting or damaging the impression.

brush. Once the ridge detail in the fingerprint is clear and sufficiently developed, do not continue to apply the brush to the print in an attempt to improve the fingerprint. The more the brush is applied to the fingerprint, the greater the chances are of smearing or distorting the ridge detail within the fingerprint. Simply stop and move on to photographing and lifting the impression.

Magnetic fingerprint brushes are also available with ferrous fingerprint powders. These brushes and powders work by picking up the ferrous powder with the magnetic fingerprint brush and applying the powder to the surface being processed (Figure 9.6). This technique has a couple of advantages.

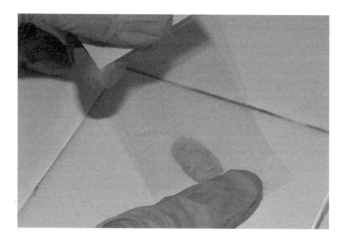

Figure 9.7 Apply the tape from one end to the other and attempt to avoid air bubbles.

Because the only thing in contact with the surface is the powder itself, the risk of the brush damaging or distorting the impression is greatly reduced, if not eliminated. Also, the powder is easily cleaned off the surface simply by moving the brush over the surface. The powder, attracted to the magnetic brush, will cling to the brush and is cleaned up very easily.

Once the fingerprint has been developed and photographed it may be lifted. Use enough tape to cover the entire fingerprint. Place one edge of the tape down beyond the edge of the fingerprint and, using your finger, press the tape down over the fingerprint, attempting to prevent any air bubbles under the tape (Figure 9.7). With practice you will be able to avoid air bubbles and creases in the tape. Remove the tape by pulling straight up. Pulling back at a sharp angle may cause the tape to curl up onto itself. Apply the tape to a fingerprint backing card using the same end-to-end technique to avoid air bubbles and creases. The tape lift should be placed on the glossy side of the card. Cut away any loose ends of the tape, such as an end that was folded to provide a leader, or if the tape has a paper tab, remove the tab and make sure that the entire piece of tape is adhering to the card. This will prevent the tape from adhering to any packaging and getting unwittingly removed from the card.

Every fingerprint lift needs to have some crucial information noted on the card. This information will be beneficial to the fingerprint examiner in the crime lab, and to the first responder who lifted the fingerprint. In many cases it may be years before the case ever goes to a hearing or trial. The notes the first responder makes on the card will be of great benefit in remembering the surface the fingerprint was developed and lifted from. If the first responder is not sure of where the fingerprint came from, it may not be admitted in court.

First responders should place their initials on the front of the card overlapping onto the tape and the card, as depicted in Figure 9.8. This will serve

Figure 9.8 The front of a fingerprint backing card; note the initials overlapping onto the tape and an orientation arrow.

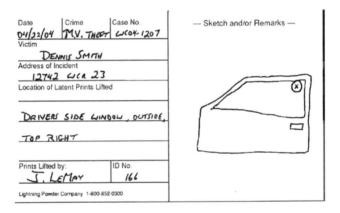

Figure 9.9 The completed fingerprint backing card.

much like signing an evidence packaging seal, as it will assure first responders when they are in court that the lift they are looking at is the same one they lifted at the scene. It is also helpful to the fingerprint examiner to place an arrow indicating which direction was up, orienting the fingerprint onto the surface it was lifted from. There are many commercially available fingerprint backing cards that have blank spaces to fill in on back of the card. These can be helpful to the first responder in remembering what information needs to be on the card. This information should include the case number, the date of recovery, the location the fingerprint was found, a rough sketch or diagram showing where the fingerprint was found, and the first responder's initials and badge number (Figure 9.9).

In some instances, if the officer is not wearing gloves when lifting fingerprints with adhesive tape, the officer's own fingerprint may be placed on the adhesive side of the tape. When this happens, simply draw an X over the impression of the officer's fingerprint. This will alert the fingerprint examiner that the print is of the collecting officer and need not be entered into the fingerprint database(s).

Photographing Fingerprints

Once the fingerprint has been developed, and prior to lifting, the fingerprint should be photographed. If a mistake is made during the lifting process, damaging the fingerprint, or if the developed fingerprint simply will not or cannot be lifted, the photographs may be the best evidence or the only evidence. Photographs should include overall and midrange photographs to establish the fingerprint's location within the scene or on a surface. Close-up photographs should be taken without a scale and with a scale. The photograph taken without a scale will show the fingerprint in its natural state and that the scale placed in the proceeding photograph is not covering any other fingerprints or other evidence.

If possible, the close-up photographs should be taken with the camera on a tripod to eliminate any camera shake and provide the sharpest possible picture. The camera should be at a ninety degree angle, perpendicular to the surface the fingerprint is on. Get as close to the fingerprint as the focus of your camera will allow and attempt to fill the frame with the fingerprint.

Automated Fingerprint Identification System (AFIS)

There are a variety of local, state, and federal databases containing the known fingerprints of millions of individuals. These databases can provide aid to fingerprint examiners in determining the source of a friction ridge impression. Your local crime lab may have access to a variety of databases it can search to attempt to determine who left fingerprints at the crime scene and provide an investigative lead into the case.

Whenever fingerprints are recovered from a crime scene they should be submitted to the crime lab to determine if they are of suitable quality and quantity to be compared and entered into an Automated Fingerprint Identification System (AFIS). If they are, then the fingerprint examiner can enter them and search against the database(s) population of millions (Figure 9.10).

Elimination prints may also be provided to the crime lab when fingerprints are recovered from a crime scene off a commonly touched source. For example, if a fingerprint is recovered off the driver's side door of a stolen car, that fingerprint could have been deposited by the vehicle owner prior to it being stolen. If known fingerprints of the vehicle owner are provided, the fingerprint examiner can first compare the fingerprint to the known prints of the car owner. If the fingerprint was made by the car owner, then there would be no need for the fingerprint examiner to enter the fingerprint into a database.

Figure 9.10 A fingerprint examiner searches a crime scene impression in an AFIS.

Figure 9.11 A fingerprint developed on paper with ninhydrin, a chemical that reacts with amino acids in fingerprint residue.

Porous Items

Porous items, such as paper, cardboard, and unfinished wood, are difficult to process with conventional fingerprint powders. Fingerprint powder may work on these types of surfaces to some degree, but there are chemicals that the forensic lab can use that are preferred methods to conventional powders (Figure 9.11). When porous evidence items, such as forged checks, threatening or harassing notes, or other documents, need to be processed for fingerprints, it may be preferred to submit them to the forensic lab rather than attempt to process them in the field. If processing in the field is the only option, a magnetic brush and powder may provide better results than a conventional brush and powder.

Controlled Substances

10

Controlled substances can be involved in nearly any criminal investigation. Cases varying from simple traffic infractions, DUI, theft, burglary, robbery, assault, sexual assault, and murder can all involve legal and illegal drugs. The illegal distribution, possession, and abuse of controlled substances in the United States is perhaps the most pressing problem facing law enforcement agencies, because so much other criminal activity is influenced by drugs. Abusers will commit thefts, burglaries, robberies, and prostitution to finance their addictions. Distributors will commit crimes such as assaults and murders to "collect" on debts. Many of the problems confronted by law enforcement agencies and judicial districts can all be related to the illegal possession, distribution, and abuse of controlled substances.

Some cases may involve legal controlled substances used in an illegal fashion. A driving under the influence case may involve a person who took a drug legally prescribed to him or her, but then drove under the effects of the drug. Prescription drugs may be abused by an individual the drug was not prescribed to. Minors have been known to take drugs from the medicine cabinet at home and abuse them or even sell them in schools. No matter the type of case, controlled substances may be a factor.

Documentation

As with any type of evidence, controlled substances found to be evidence in a case must be thoroughly documented in photographs, notes, diagrams, and reports. The drugs should be photographed in place as they were found. Notes should be made as to their location, condition, and quantity. If a scene sketch is produced, the location of the drugs should be included. And all of this detail must be included in the officer's report. As with any type of evidence, if its location condition and quantity are not documented, the evidence may be dismissed and the case could be lost.

If the drug is in a pill form, a count of the number of pills should be made. This count should be performed in the presence of another officer to witness the quantity of the drug. The count should be documented on a form or evidence sheet with the submitting officer's signature and the initials or signature

Figure 10.1 A substance to be weighed is left in its packaging, and the weight will include the substance and the packaging.

of the officer who witnessed the count. Having another officer witness the pill count may help the submitting officer and the agency if accused of some impropriety. After counting, the pills should be returned to the container in which they were found. The container with the pills should then be packaged, sealed, and submitted according to agency policies and procedures.

If the controlled substance is in something other than pill form, the weight of the substance should be determined. The loose substance should not be removed from its container but should be weighed in the packaging in which it was found (Figure 10.1). This will prevent any from being accidentally lost or misplaced. If the substance is found wrapped in cellophane packaging it should be weighed in the cellophane packaging, and it should be noted in the report that the weight includes the substance and the cellophane packaging.

If the substance is a plant material, such as marijuana or marijuana plants, it should be packaged in paper rather than plastic. In plastic, moisture from the plants will not be allowed to evaporate and will cause mildew. This will degrade the material. If the material is found in a plastic package, leave it in that packaging, but after weighing put the plastic package and its contents in a paper package.

Dogs have a very acute sense of smell and can be trained in the detection of drugs. They can search large areas with poor visibility and that may be concealed completely from view, such as hidden compartments in cars. Even attempts to mask odors from drug-sniffing dogs are unsuccessful because dogs can detect multiple odors at a time. The assistance of a drug detection canine can be of great benefit in the search for controlled substances.

Drug Identification

There are many different types of illicit drugs sold on the street. The ability to recognize and perform field tests on them is imperative to the first responder. Not having the knowledge of the different types of illicit drugs and what they look like may result in them being overlooked. Without the ability to field test drugs, a police officer may mistakenly arrest someone for possession of a controlled substance when in fact it may be something perfectly legal and benign.

Marijuana is intended for use as a psychoactive drug. It is most commonly used in a dried herbal form (Figures 10.2 to 10.4). The main psychoactive compound in marijuana is tetrahydrocannabinol (THC). Consuming marijuana causes psychoactive and physiological effects. It can change a person's mood with hallucinogenic or psychedelic effects and can increase heart rate; lower blood pressure; and impair memory, coordination, and concentration.

Cocaine is a highly addictive stimulant of the central nervous system and an appetite suppressant. It is derived from the leaves of the coca plant and commonly has a white "pearly" appearance. It can be in a compressed brick form or powder (Figure 10.5 and Figure 10.6). It is frequently adulterated or "cut" with common products such as sugars or baking soda and can also be cut with other stimulants such as methamphetamine.

Cocaine may be orally ingested by rubbing along the gum line, rubbed onto a cigarette filter and smoked, or wrapped in rolling paper and swallowed. It can be snorted and then absorbed through the mucous membrane in the sinuses. It can be melted and injected.

Figure 10.2 Dried flowers from the marijuana plant.

Figure 10.3 Dried flowers from the marijuana plant. Note the trichomes, or glistening crystals, that contain large quantities of THC.

Figure 10.4 Marijuana plants are often cultivated for illicit personal use or sale. The long leaves have a sawtooth-type edge.

Cocaine's effects are increased alertness and feeling of well-being and euphoria. It increases energy and motor activity and also can result in anxiety, restlessness, and paranoia.

Heroin is derived from opium poppies. It can be found in a white crystalline form, a chunky brown form, or a sticky black tar (Figure 10.7). It is extremely addictive and has a high potential for abuse. It can be injected in veins or muscles, snorted, or smoked.

Figure 10.5 Cocaine in compressed brick and powder form. It may be sold in chunks from the brick or in powder form.

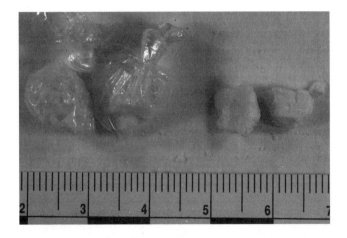

Figure 10.6 Crack cocaine packaged in quantities of two-tenths of a gram ready for distribution. The user may get two or three uses out of this quantity.

Heroin causes feelings of transcendent relaxation and intense euphoria. Tolerance develops quickly and the user needs more of the drug to achieve the same effects. A heroin user may display alternating alertness and drowsiness. Heroin can also result in muscle weakness. Large doses of it can cause fatal respiratory depression, and accidental overdoses can occur. The drug has also been used in suicides and homicides.

Methamphetamine (meth) is a stimulant drug. It may be in a crystalline form or an off-white crumbly block (Figure 10.8). It increases energy and alertness and can induce euphoria, anxiety, sociability, irritability, aggression, and paranoia; enhance self-esteem; and increase sexual pleasure. It has

Figure 10.7 Black tar heroin.

Figure 10.8 Crystal methamphetamine. Meth may be found in crystalline form or in an off-white crumbly block.

a high potential for abuse. Meth abusers have been known to stay awake for several days and then sleep for several days. Abuse of meth may result in premature loss of the teeth, lack of or ignoring personal hygiene, and obsessive picking at the skin, which can lead to abscesses.

Intravenous injection may be the most common method of administration, but meth can also be swallowed, snorted, smoked, or inserted anally or vaginally.

Prior to the 1990s meth was commonly manufactured by drug distributors in Mexico and California. Since then clandestine production has become widespread throughout the United States. Recipes can be easily found on the Internet, and the materials needed to produce it can be purchased or stolen from drug stores and hardware and automotive stores. Meth labs can be very simple and unsophisticated operations that can be placed in a box and moved easily from location to location. They can be recognized by the presence of glass cooking ware, plastic tubing, large amounts of over-the-counter drugs containing ephedrine or pseudoephedrine, products containing red phosphorous, iodine, lantern fuel, hydrochloric acid, battery acid, lye, and antifreeze.

Upon encountering a clandestine lab, the first responder should evacuate the immediate area and call for assistance. Meth labs can contain toxic and explosive gases. Untrained personnel without the proper personal protective equipment should never attempt to dismantle, process, or collect a clandestine lab.

Ecstasy, or MDMA (3,4-Methylenedioxymethamphetamine), has become a popular recreational drug in the United States in recent decades. Taken orally in pill form or powder form, or snorted in powder form, ecstasy can cause extreme mood lift with accompanying euphoria (Figure 10.9). It can cause a strong sense of inner peace and improved self-confidence. Chronic use can lead to depression, liver damage, excessive wear of the teeth, and central nervous system damage.

LSD (lysergic acid diethylamide) is a psychedelic drug well known for its psychological effects. It can cause altered thinking processes and hallucinations. It is typically delivered orally from a substrate such as blotter paper placed on the tongue (Figure 10.10), a sugar cube, or gelatin. In liquid form it can also be injected. LSD may cause an altered experience of awareness, time, emotions, senses, and memories. It may include dramatic visual effects such as the movement of static surfaces, trails of moving objects, and an intensification of colors and brightness. Use may result in impairment of judgment and understanding of common dangers, making the user more susceptible to accidents and personal injury.

The use of mushrooms containing the hallucinogenic psilocybin dates back millennium (Figure 10.11). The mushrooms are ingested by various methods and are nontoxic. The effects can vary from user to user and may last from three to eight hours. Physical effects of the psychedelic drug are increased heart rate and blood pressure, increased energy and feelings of well-being, reduction in stress, and muscle relaxation. There can be increased visual activity such as surfaces that seem to ripple, shimmer, or breathe. A negative environment may result in a "bad trip," whereas a pleasant environment may result in a pleasant experience.

Peyote is a small spineless cactus that is native to Southwestern Texas and Central Mexico. It contains a psychoactive alkaloid called mescaline.

(a)   (b)

(c)   (d)

(e)

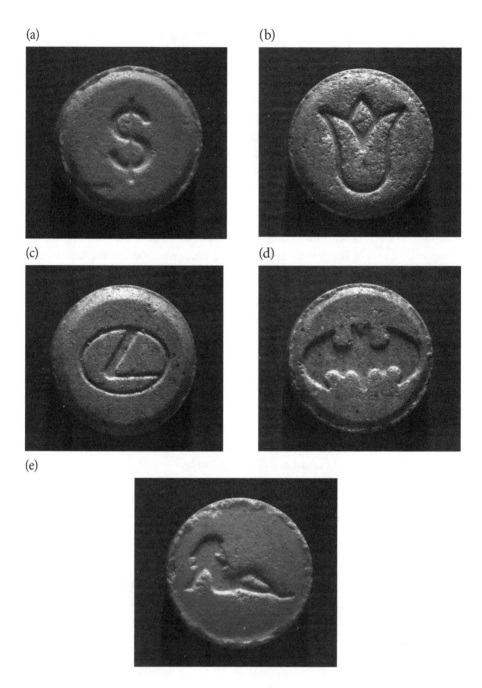

Figure 10.9 Ecstasy pills with various figures stamped in them. Ecstasy pills may be found in a variety of shapes and colors. Ecstasy may be taken orally or snorted in powder form. (Courtesy of Matthew Jorgenson.)

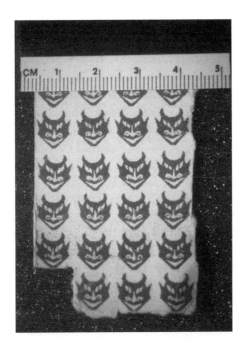

Figure 10.10 LSD blotter paper. A blotter is placed on the tongue and the drug is absorbed. (Courtesy of Matthew Jorgenson.)

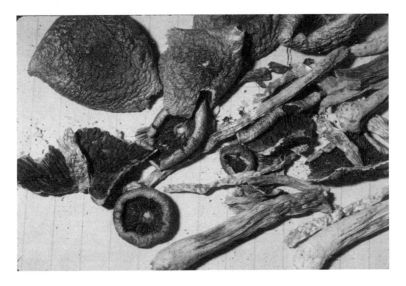

Figure 10.11 Psilocybin mushrooms are ingested orally and may have psyche-delic or hallucinogenic effects. (Courtesy of Matthew Jorgenson.)

The cactus' disc-shaped buttons are cut above the roots and are sometimes dried (Figure 10.12). The buttons are then chewed or boiled in water to make a tea (Figure 10.13). Peyote is reported to trigger states of deep introspection and insight described as spiritual or metaphysical in nature.

Anabolic steroids increase protein synthesis within cells, which results in the buildup of muscle tissue. In the presence of an adequate diet, taking anabolic steroids can result in increases in lean muscle mass and muscle strength. Health risks associated are harmful changes in cholesterol levels, acne, high blood pressure, liver damage, and dangerous changes in the structure of the left ventricle of the heart. Significant psychological side effects such as increased aggression, violence, and mania, also known as "roid rage," may be encountered with the steroid abuser. Anabolic steroids may be taken in oral pills, injectable steroids (Figure 10.14), and skin patches. Injection is the most common method for individuals administering anabolic steroids for nonmedical purposes.

Field Tests

Field tests for controlled substances are available commercially. These are extremely useful to the law enforcement officers in the field who have encountered an unknown substance or a substance they suspect is illicit. When an individual is found in the possession of a white powder, it is important to be

Figure 10.12 Peyote buttons. Peyote is an extremely slow growing cactus that takes years to go from seedling to mature flowering adult. (Courtesy of Matthew Jorgenson.)

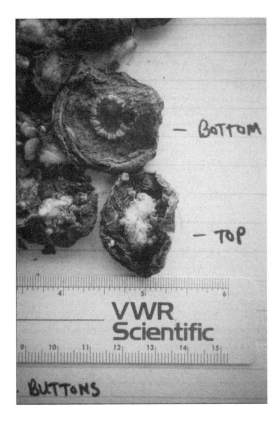

Figure 10.13 Dried peyote buttons, which may be chewed or boiled in water to make a tea. (Courtesy of Matthew Jorgenson.)

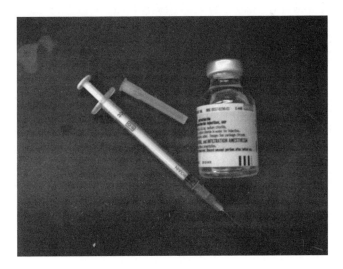

Figure 10.14 A vial of injectable anabolic steroids. (Courtesy of Matthew Jorgenson.)

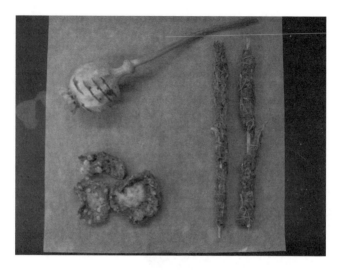

Figure 10.15 (Clockwise from top) An opium poppy that has been cut to extract the heroin; Thai sticks, which are a form of marijuana consisting of premium buds of seedless marijuana skewered on stems; and peyote buttons. (Courtesy of Matthew Jorgenson.)

able to identify that white powder as quickly as possible so that charges may or may not be brought upon the individual. Substances may be found in a variety of forms, i.e., an opium poppy that has been cut to extract heroin, or thai sticks that are a form of marijuana consisting of premium buds of seedless marijuana skewered on stems (Figure 10.15). Field tests allow for the immediate presumptive testing of that material, however, they are only presumptive and not absolutely conclusive. Positive results from a field test typically provide sufficient probable cause for an arrest and charges to be filed. But an actual definitive determination of the makeup of the substance must be performed by a forensic chemist in the crime lab.

Field tests are easy to use, but the instructions must be followed completely. Field tests that are used incorrectly can result in false-positive test results. If the wrong test is used or it is used incorrectly, it may result in an innocent person being arrested or a guilty person being set free.

A commonly used field test kit includes a small transparent plastic pouch with small glass ampoules inside. A small sample of the unknown substance is placed in the pouch and, per the test kit instructions, the ampoules are broken in order and the pouch is agitated to mix the chemicals with the unknown substance. A color change or color separation is observed in the liquid in the pouch, which shows a presumptive positive or negative result.

330 results for white, Round pills marked with M were found.

Page: < Back 13 14 15 16 17 Next >

Images licensed from GOLD STANDARD ELSEVIER

	Drug Name	Strength	Markings	Maker / Distributor
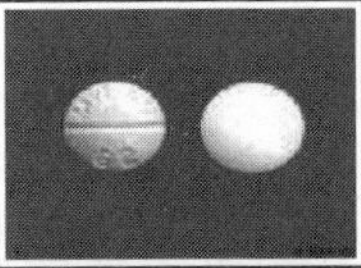	Glipizide	10 mg	MYLAN G2	Mylan Pharmaceuticals Inc
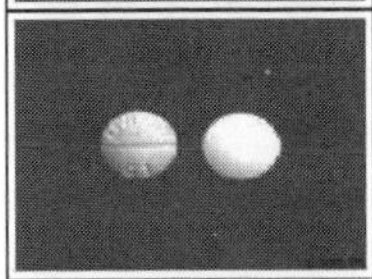	Glipizide	5 mg	MYLAN G1	Mylan Pharmaceuticals Inc
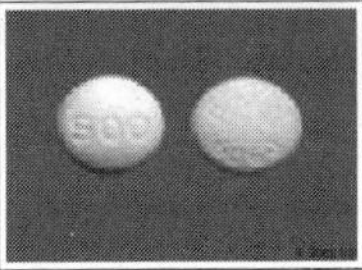	Glucophage	500 mg	BMS 6060 / 500	Bristol Myers Squibb Co

Figure 10.16 A screenshot from www.healthline.com/pillfinder. By entering the color, shape, and markings on the pill, the tool identifies pills with those characteristics.

Prescription Drug Identification

At times the first responder will encounter loose prescription drugs in an unmarked container, or multiple prescriptions or over-the-counter drugs in one container. It is naturally difficult to determine if the person possessing the drugs is in possession of them legally when it is undetermined what the drugs are.

The *Physicians' Desk Reference* (*PDR*) is an authoritative source of Food and Drug Administration (FDA)-approved information on prescription drugs. It is a comprehensive and user-friendly resource for more than 2400 drugs. When an unknown prescription drug is encountered or seized, the *PDR* is a source to identify the drug. The pills can be researched by color, shape, and markings.

There are also Web sites that can be helpful resources. For example, www.healthline.com/pillfinder has you enter the color of the pill, the shape, and the markings on the pill, and it will provide you with photographs, drug name, markings, and maker or distributor of the drug (Figure 10.16).

Death Scene Investigation

11

"Every scene, every time." That is the advice from the National Institute of Justice in a published research report titled *National Guidelines for Death Investigation*.[*] Investigating the scene of a death is crucial in determining the cause and manner of death. The results of the scene investigation may have obvious criminal implications in a homicide investigation. But there may also be vital findings in an accidental death, natural death, or suicide. Evidence gathered or neglected at the scene may have implications into civil matters related to life insurance, workers' compensation benefits, wrongful deaths, occupational safety issues, and much more. I have been subpoenaed in several noncriminal death investigations to appear at civil hearings and trials.

"How local death investigators do their job at a death investigation is crucial to family members who are mourning a loss today and who may be seeking justice tomorrow," wrote Jeanne M. Adkins, a representative of the Colorado State Legislature.[†] These words do not just pertain to criminal cases. I have experienced accidental death cases where insurance companies have refused to pay death benefits to the insured's family, claiming that the death was not an accident but a suicide. In such cases, if evidence at the death scene is neglected, the truth about the incident may be clouded, and the courts, not receiving all of the facts about the case, may be forced into unfavorable rulings for families seeking some consolation after the loss of a loved one.

If a body is found at the bottom of a staircase, ask: Did the victim trip and fall (an accidental death)? Did the victim suffer a heart attack at the top of the stairs and then fall (natural death)? Did the victim throw himself or herself down the stairs to end some form of suffering (suicide)? Was the victim pushed down the stairs (homicide)?[‡]

Only the fourth explanation involves criminal activity. However, because the investigation must determine whether the case was a homicide, the other possibilities must be investigated. If a death scene appears to be noncriminal

---

[*] U.S. Department of Justice, Office of Justice Programs, National Institute of Justice, National Guidelines for Death Investigation, December 1997.

[†] U.S. Department of Justice, National Guidelines for Death Investigation, "Foreword Commentary."

[‡] Wayne W. Bennett and Kären M. Hess, *Criminal Investigation*, 7th ed. (Belmont, CA: Thomson Wadsworth, 2004).

in nature, the manner of death cannot be taken for granted. There have been cases where the initial appearance of a death is natural or accidental, only to have a small bullet wound, blunt force wound, or knife wound found later at an autopsy. If hours, days, or weeks have lapsed since the scene was initially processed and released, it may be impossible to return to the scene to document and collect evidence. In some cases of homicide, the killer may attempt to disguise the scene to appear to be a suicide or accident. Regardless of the initial appearance of a scene, it is important to take nothing for granted and always process the scene thoroughly and professionally.

It is important to recognize that every case worked, whether criminal or not, needs to be investigated thoroughly. Every call that the first responder services receive may result in criminal or civil proceedings and require thorough scene investigation.

Cause and Manner of Death

The cause and manner of death are determined by the pathologist. The manners in which a person may die are homicide, suicide, accident, and natural. In some cases the manner of death is undetermined. If the pathologist cannot be certain if the mechanism that caused the death was performed by another, self-inflicted, an accident, or a natural occurrence, then the cause of death is ruled to be undetermined. Homicide is simply defined as the taking of one human life by another. Homicide, in many cases, is justified. Homicide cases involving self-defense or defense of a third party are often deemed to be justified and are not criminal in nature.

Cause of death is the mechanism by which a person's life is ended. It can be various types of trauma, poisoning, hypo- or hyperthermia, or any of a multitude of natural causes. It is important not to make assumptions at the crime scene with regard to cause of death. An erroneous assumption as to the cause of death could lead an investigation down a wrong path and may jeopardize the ultimate solution of a crime. For example, if a stab wound is mistaken for a gunshot wound the entire investigation could be sidetracked.[*] First responders and investigators need to rely on the expertise of the forensic pathologist in determining cause and manner of death and not make bold assumptions at the scene.

When describing injuries in notes and reports, it is important to be general in the descriptions. Avoid terms such as "gunshot wound" or "knife wound." Instead use general terms such as "round-shaped wound" or "linear-shaped wound." The skin stretches in different directions and at different angles in

[*] Barry A. J. Fisher, *Techniques of Crime Scene Investigation*, 5th ed. (Boca Raton, FL: CRC Press, 1993), Chapter 5.

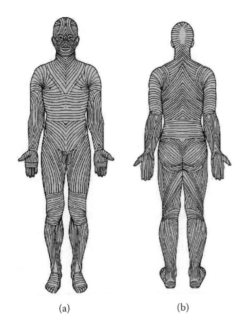

(a)   (b)

Figure 11.1 Lines of Langer show the different directions skin stretches across the body. This stretching can make a slitlike wound from a stabbing appear round or a round wound such as from a gunshot appear linear.

different areas of the body. This has been researched and is known as lines of Langer (Figure 11.1). Skin can stretch and make round wounds, such as gunshot wounds, appear linear in shape, and knife wounds can sometimes appear round in shape. If the officer reports a wound as a knife wound and the pathologist reports it as a gunshot wound, not only may the officer's credibility be challenged, it may result in the inadmissibility of evidence.

Jurisdiction over the Body

First responders need to become familiar with the laws in their states or provinces regarding the handling and jurisdiction of a corpse. In many states a body, or anything on or near a body, may not be touched without first consulting with the coroner or medical examiner. The position of the body and the presence and condition of items on or near the body may be crucial to the coroner or medical examiner in determining cause and manner of death. If the body or those items on or near the body are disturbed, it could jeopardize the investigation. If a victim is obviously deceased and there is no need to render aid, then the body and items on or near the body should not be disturbed.

Actions such as removing a wallet from a victim's pocket to obtain an identification card or removing a weapon from a scene not only may be in violation of the law but may expose the officer and his or her agency to civil liability. If weapons or other items must be secured for scene safety reasons, the actions and the reasons for those actions taken must be thoroughly documented.

Postmortem Lividity

When the heart stops beating, the blood begins to be drawn into the lower portions of the body due to gravity. The result is the lower portions of the body will have a reddish-brown appearance. This is known as postmortem lividity, or livor mortis. This discoloration begins immediately after death and will be fully developed within three to four hours. It should not be confused with bruising, and a pathologist can tell the difference between the two at autopsy. Low areas of skin that are in contact with a surface will not fill with blood. The pressure on the skin will prevent the blood from pooling in those blood vessels (Figure 11.2). In cases where the victim lost a large amount of blood, livor mortis may not be apparent or may not fully develop. Lividity in cases of carbon monoxide deaths will have a bright, cherry red color.

The degree and extent of the discoloration may be an aid in the determination of time of death. They may also demonstrate the change of position or movement of a body several hours after death.* If the body is positioned on its back, and there is lividity on the chest, this may indicate that the body was

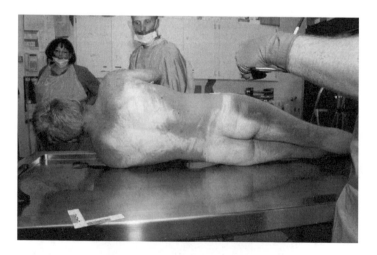

Figure 11.2 Redness on the back indicates that this body was positioned on its back after death. Note the areas of white skin where the skin was in contact with the ground, preventing blood from filling those blood vessels.

* Ibid.

originally laying face down and at some point was rolled over onto its back. The first responder should be aware of the possibility that the body was moved and the crime scene was altered or staged to appear to be something it is not.

Rigor Mortis

Rigor mortis, or rigidity of the body, is due to biochemical changes in the body, which result in the stiffening of the muscles. This first appears two to six hours after death and may first be apparent in the muscles of the jaw and neck, and then move to the torso and extremities. In full rigor mortis the body is extremely stiff and it can be very difficult to move or reposition the extremities (Figure 11.3a and Figure 11.3b). It can be complete within six to twelve hours and may remain for two to three days, after which the muscles will "relax."

There are factors that can affect the onset and duration of rigor mortis, such as the musculature of the victim and whether the victim was under some physical stress at the time of death. Climate conditions may also affect the onset and release of rigor mortis.

Rigor mortis may be used as an aid in establishing the time of death. It may also be used by the first responder at the scene in determining if a body

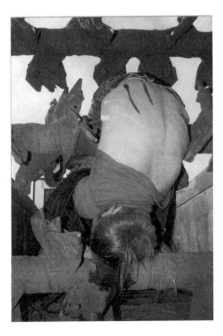

Figure 11.3a This accident victim was found approximately twelve hours after death in this position.

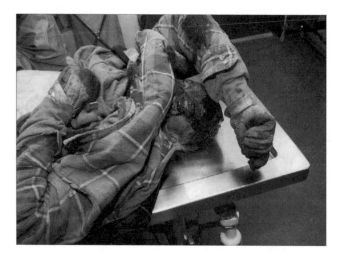

Figure 11.3b Due to rigor mortis the arms are locked in position over the victim's head and could not be moved.

has been moved or if a scene has been staged. If a body is positioned on its back and an extremity is raised off the ground in rigor mortis, this may indicate that this extremity was not in this position originally, and the body has been moved.

Scene Documentation

Take overall photographs of the scene, and midrange and close-up photographs of evidence within the scene. Include all details in notes and sketches. Photograph the body from all angles to show its position in the scene, the condition of clothing, and the locations of any objects on or near the body. Take close-up photographs of the decedent's face and any scars, marks, tattoos, or injuries that may be visible on scene. More detailed documentation of the victim's injuries will be performed later at the autopsy. Take additional photographs after objects have been removed from on or around the body. After the body has been removed, photograph the surface underneath the body to show the absence or presence of any evidence or the absence or presence of any bloodstains under the body.

If a firearm was used in the incident, it may be desirable to use a gunshot residue collection kit. This collection may be done at the scene or later at the autopsy. If this is to be done on scene, be sure to consult with the investigator from the coroner's office or medical examiner's office prior to the collection being performed.

Law Enforcement's Role at Autopsy

The role of law enforcement at an autopsy is a limited one. The autopsy is performed by the pathologist, who may be assisted by a medicolegal death investigator or an autopsy technician. The law enforcement representative may take photographs of the body and external and internal injuries. The face, tattoos, and scars or marks should be photographed for identification purposes. The officer will receive evidence that is collected by the pathologist. All items of clothing the decedent is wearing, if collected, should each be packaged in a separate paper bag. If the items are wet or bloody they may be placed in plastic bags for transport to the law enforcement agency and immediately placed in an air-dry facility to be thoroughly air-dried before finally being packaged in paper.

The pathologist may collect other evidence from the body such as from sexual assault examination kits and gunshot residue kits, fingernail scrapings, fingerprints of the decedent, blood blotter cards, bullets, or other foreign objects. These items must be cataloged to show the origination of the chain of custody and submitted to the law enforcement agency's evidence unit.

Metallic objects such as bullets, lead fragments, or copper bullet jackets that are recovered from the body at autopsy should be thoroughly rinsed with water and dried prior to packaging and submission. Blood left on these items may cause decay and corrosion, resulting in loss of detail-like striations or rifling on a bullet imparted from the firearm barrel.

At the autopsy the pathologist may discuss the medical findings of the examination. The pathologist may discuss injuries and cause and manner of death with law enforcement representatives present at the autopsy. It is important for officers at the autopsy to resist reporting the medical findings. Leave reporting the medical findings up to the medical expert. If officers try to describe medical findings in their report with the lack of medical expertise of a pathologist, it is possible that they may report the findings incorrectly and their report may contradict that of the pathologist. This will impact the credibility of the officers. Never stick your neck out by reporting things that should only be reported by an expert.

Courtroom Presentation and Testimony 12

Testifying in the courtroom is one of the most important duties of the law enforcement professional. It is where all of the hard work spent on a case comes to fruition. It is when first responders get their chance to tell a judge and jury about what they observed and did in a case, and how and why they did it. A defendant's life and liberty is at stake, and also at stake may be the professional credibility and reputation of the law enforcement professional.

Yet, with so much on the line, many law enforcement professionals go their entire career with little or no training or instruction in courtroom testimony. There are training courses and instructional books available on the subject, but for some reason, some law enforcement professionals seem to take courtroom testimony for granted. There is always great emphasis on training in subjects such as firearms, defensive and pursuit driving, self-defense, and criminal law, as there certainly should be. But testifying in court is an essential and unavoidable duty of the first responder. And each and every one of us could benefit from a little study or training on the subject.

It is natural to be nervous when testifying in court. There can be great pressure felt by the witness. The judge, jury, attorneys, court reporter, and the gallery are paying close attention to every word spoken. A person's life and liberty may also be hanging in the balance. The pressure felt emphasizes the great responsibility of the law enforcement professional. Public speaking is also one of the most common fears, and it is important that the first responder find ways to become comfortable with public speaking. Speak to civic groups or at schools, citizen academies, or any function that may provide an opportunity. Talking to people about what you do, how you do it, and why you do it is much like what you will do in court. Public speaking opportunities can be great practice for courtroom testimony.

Preparation and Pretrial Conference

Once the law enforcement professional receives a subpoena to appear in court, the preparation should begin. In many cases it may be months or years since you, the first responder, last worked on or even thought about the case. Memories fade, and even if a case were a memorable one, details may be forgotten and you need time to review all the reports, notes, and the evidence you submitted in the case. You should review all photographs and diagrams. Also ensure you are aware of the appearance of evidence collected, where it was located, how it was documented and collected, and what was done with it. It may be necessary to remove evidence from storage and examine it again just to refamiliarize yourself with it so that you will recognize it when it is handed to you in the courtroom.

Contact the lawyer who is requesting your appearance in court and request a pretrial conference. Prosecuting attorneys can be very busy people, and it may be difficult to get a meeting with them, but it is crucial that the first responder be as prepared as possible before entering the courtroom, and a discussion with the prosecutor can help you get prepared. Be persistent in your attempts to contact them. Find out what evidence the attorney will introduce in court through you and find out what questions they will ask you about that evidence. If you have concerns over any issues or you are aware that there may be difficult issues with any of the evidence, be sure to point those issues out to the attorneys so that they can be prepared and are not surprised or embarrassed in court.

If you are subpoenaed by the defense in a case, extend the defense attorneys the same professional courtesy as the prosecutor. Attempt to contact them and request a pretrial conference. Find out why they are requesting your appearance in court. Find out what evidence, if any, that they want to introduce in court through you. And find out what questions they intend to ask you in court. By extending the same professional courtesy to the defense as you would the prosecution, you demonstrate that you are unbiased and objective in the investigation.

Find out from the attorneys if they want you to bring any of the evidence into court with you. Miscommunication can occur when the attorneys believe the witness is bringing the evidence to court, and the witness believes the attorneys will bring the evidence to court. Make sure you know ahead of time what the expectation is to avoid any last-minute scramble to get the evidence from its storage location to court.

If you are appearing in a courtroom that you have never been in before, take some time before your appearance to familiarize yourself with how to get there and the floor plan of the courtroom. First impressions mean a lot, and if you enter the courtroom looking lost about where to go and what to do, you may damage your image with the jury. Learn where the witness stand is and where the jury sits. Learn if there is a gate to walk through and find out which way it swings. Try sitting in the witness seat and make sure you fit in it comfortably with your Sam Browne belt on if you have to wear it in court. Find out if the chair squeaks if you swivel side to side. This preparation will help you look confident and professional and make a good first impression on the jury. This familiarity may also help ease some of the tension you will feel before you enter the courtroom to testify.

Courtroom Dress and Demeanor

Image is everything. There is a great deal of truth to this axiom. Jurors, like any members of society, may draw certain conclusions about you based on your appearance. The law enforcement professional in court is being judged by the jury. Jurors have a very important decision to make regarding the guilt or innocence of the defendant, and they want to know that the people presenting evidence to them are credible and professional. A witness who appears sloppy and unprofessional won't impress a jury.

Your department may have policies regarding what you can and cannot wear in court, and you should always follow those policies. If your department policy mandates that you wear your uniform in court, avoid wearing any additional uniform decorations that may be a distraction to the jury. Leave off the unnecessary pins, ribbons, and whistles. If it is difficult for you to get in and out of the witness chair with your Sam Browne belt on, leave it off too.

If you are going to wear civilian clothes, dress professionally and conservative. A good tip I received once was to dress like the news anchors on television. Men should wear suits or a blazer and tie. Wear a conservative tie and don't choose one with any distracting patterns. Wearing a tie with images of things like baseballs or hot sauce bottles may appear unprofessional and may distract jurors from what they need to be paying attention to. Don't wear a lapel pin that may represent an organization or something you may feel proud about. It may represent something that may offend a juror. Hair and facial hair should be clean and neatly trimmed. Men should avoid wearing earrings. Although many in society accept men wearing earrings, some do not and they may be sitting on the jury. Don't take any chances when it comes to earning the jurors' respect.

Women should dress in conservative and professional business suits. Again, modeling after local television news anchors is a safe way to choose a wardrobe for court. Earrings should be coordinated with the outfit and should not be too large, dangling, or distracting.

Every witness should avoid heavy perfumes, colognes, and aftershaves. A strong scent may be offensive to a juror, and a juror may even be allergic to it. Just don't forget the antiperspirant.

When testifying it is important to acknowledge the jury. Look at the questioning attorney while he or she is asking a question and then turn and address the jury when answering. Attempt to make eye contact with each juror during testimony. They are the ones in the courtroom with the heavy burden of deciding guilty or not guilty. They have had to take time off from work or time away from their family to be there. They may be losing pay or making other personal sacrifices to attend jury duty, and they will appreciate you addressing them directly and looking them in the eye. If you are asked a series of questions that only require a yes or no answer, it is not necessary to turn your head each time to look at the jury. But if the answer requires more than a simple yes or no response, turn to the jurors and look them in the eye while you speak.

If the proceeding is a trial before a judge only and no jury is present, or if the proceeding is a preliminary hearing or motion hearing before a judge, direct your answers to the judge. In these proceedings it is the judge who will be making a decision regarding probable cause or evidence admissibility, and you should look the judge in the eye and pay him or her due respect. The judge may be taking notes or looking at legal references, so don't be bothered if the judge is not looking at you. But judges may appreciate it when they do look at you and you are speaking directly to them.

Speak slowly, clearly, and into the microphone. If you are away from a microphone speak loud enough for everyone in the courtroom to hear. The court reporter is typing everything the witnesses say, and if they speak too quickly the court reporter will have to ask the them to repeat themselves. Having to repeat your answer can be frustrating and embarrassing. It may also be difficult for the judge and jury to understand the witness's testimony if it is spoken too quickly or too softly.

Courtroom Exhibits and Displays

There are many ways evidence may be exhibited in court. Deciding which way is best may depend on the layout of the courtroom, availability of equipment, and even preferences of the presiding judge.

Digital photographs and crime scene diagrams may be presented by projecting them onto a screen, printing them, and using an overhead projection system to display them on television or flat-screen monitors. Printed photographs or diagrams may be displayed by using an overhead projection system, enlargements displayed on an easel or smaller enlargements passed from juror to juror, or multiple copies produced for each juror and the court. In many judicial districts the attorneys who want to introduce this evidence in court will have these displays prepared before the hearing or trial. But it is incumbent on witnesses to speak to the attorneys to find out how these images will be displayed and what, if any, their responsibility is in preparation before entering the courtroom.

Some evidence may present unique challenges when attempting to present them in court. Items such as bloody clothing may be difficult and messy to spread out in open court. Such evidence can be laid flat on a piece Plexiglass with another piece of Plexiglass laid on top. Seal the edges with heavy tape. Now this evidence can be safely and cleanly handled without any concern of contamination or making a mess in the courtroom. If there are holes on the clothing such as bullet holes or holes made by a knife blade, it is advisable to place a clean piece of paper inside the clothing to allow the hole to show through. Use a color of paper that contrasts well with the color of the clothing. For example, if the clothing item is a bloody black shirt with a hole in it, line the inside of the shirt with white butcher paper so the hole can be clearly seen.

Be careful handling weapons in court. If you are handed a firearm ask the judge for permission to examine it to make sure it is unloaded and in a safe condition in the interest of everyone's safety in the courtroom. This will demonstrate to the jurors your respect for dangerous weapons and your concern for their safety. They will appreciate this.

If you are asked to handle evidence it is advisable to wear a pair of protective gloves. Although there is little risk of catching anything infectious from evidence that may have been stored a long time, it again illustrates that you are conscientious about personal and public safety. Place one or two pairs of gloves in your pocket before going to court. There may be a box of gloves in the courtroom, but it may impress the jury if you bring your own. Also you know they will be the right size and you won't have to fumble with them to get them on.

Adversarial System

The American judicial system is adversarial, meaning two sides take up evidence and witnesses and argue against each other. The prosecution has the burden of proving beyond a reasonable doubt that a crime was committed and that the defendant committed the crime. The defense attempts to create a reasonable doubt in the minds of the judge and/or jury as to the defendant's guilt.

So what side does the law enforcement professional fall on in this argument? In the author's opinion, neither. Law enforcement has the burden of investigating crime. Evidence from crime scenes must be gathered objectively; information from witnesses, victims, and suspects must be gathered without bias; and information must be reported factually and completely.

Some cases present challenges in that the crime may be egregious and shocking in nature. Investigators may become emotionally attached to such a case and it may become difficult to prevent personal bias from entering into the investigation. In some cases where repeat offenders are a nuisance to law enforcement and to the community, investigators may begin to take the case personally and their determination to catch and convict the offender may blur their objectivity. While we are all human and are subject to such passion and emotion, it is important to attempt to remain emotionally detached from a case and be as objective as possible in an investigation.

The law enforcement professional does not work on the side of the prosecution or the defense. Consider yourself an advocate for the evidence and you are simply testifying to facts in the case. This is especially applicable under cross-examination from defense attorneys. Defense attorneys may use tactics to attempt to discredit the law enforcement witness. They may attempt to make it appear to the judge and jury that you were incompetent or erred in the investigation. They may even challenge your personal integrity. These tactics are not personal and may actually indicate that you did such a good job in the investigation that there are no weak points to attack, so they attack you. If you react to such tactics defensively you may only damage your credibility with the judge and jury. By remaining calm and responding rationally the tactic may backfire on the attorney and make it appear that he or she is only badgering you. This may earn you more respect and maybe even sympathy from the jury, and reflect poorly on the attorney. Simply testify to the facts of the case as you know them and be a good advocate for the evidence.

Case Studies

13

Case Number 1

Late one July afternoon, a murder occurred on the dirt driveway at a dairy farm. The victim and at least three witnesses were relaxing on the lawn outside in the shade when the suspect, who was known by the victim and had previous altercations with the victim, drove onto the property. The suspect drove past the victim and the witnesses, then parked out of sight behind a home and some trees. He then approached the victim and the witnesses carrying a .22 caliber single-shot bolt-action rifle. He confronted the victim on the dirt driveway of the property and fired one shot into the victim's head, which killed him instantly. The victim lay in the dirt driveway, face down near the edge of the lawn. The suspect fled the scene and was arrested hours later by detectives.

One of the witnesses immediately called the dairy owner who lived just down the road. The owner and his son arrived and parked in the dirt driveway just north of the victim. He then called 911 and emergency personnel began to arrive on scene. The first to arrive on scene was a local police officer from a nearby town. Then three firefighters and one paramedic arrived and entered the scene. Two more local police officers arrived and entered the scene. Four sheriff's deputies and one sheriff's office commander entered the scene and two state troopers also walked into the scene. In all there were twenty-one people in the scene, including the fourteen first responders who entered the scene and walked in the dirt driveway. In all, 143 footwear impressions were documented in the driveway (Figure 13.1). This could have been avoided had the first responders entered the scene walking on the grass rather than the dirt driveway. Had the first responders walked on the grass, the only footwear impressions in the driveway would have been those of the suspect, victim, and witnesses.

Many of the footwear impressions were overlapping, meaning that people were not paying attention to where they were stepping and stepped on top of existing footwear impressions (Figure 13.2). This may have resulted in the obliteration of footwear impressions from the suspect or witnesses. Analysis of these impressions may have helped show where individuals were standing or walking within the scene.

There were three footwear impressions on the ground immediately around the victim's body, which were made by a Magnum brand boot, which is a common boot worn by law enforcement officers (Figure 13.3a

Figure 13.1 There were 143 footwear impressions in the dirt driveway, which were marked and photographed using overall, midrange, and close-up examination-quality photography techniques.

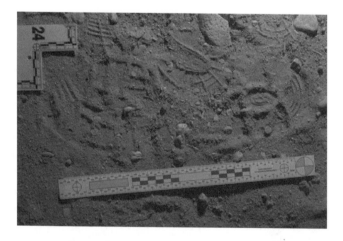

Figure 13.2 Many of the footwear impressions in the scene were overlapping, meaning that people were stepping on top of existing footwear impressions in the scene.

and Figure 13.3b). None of the twenty-one people who were known to have been in the scene were wearing Magnum boots. This suggests that there was another first responder in the scene who was unaccounted for. Every person who appeared on the crime scene entry log and every person who appeared on the dispatch log was contacted; none of them were wearing Magnum brand boots. This means that someone entered the scene and inspected the body and is completely unaccounted for.

Figure 13.3a A footwear impression near the victim's body, which was made by a Magnum brand boot. No one who is accounted for in the scene was wearing a Magnum brand boot.

Figure 13.3b The outsole of a Magnum brand boot, which corresponds in outsole design to the boot that made the three impressions around the victim's body.

The crime scene diagrams illustrate the large number of footwear impressions within the scene. Tire impressions were also documented at the driveway entrance to the property. In addition, other evidence documented was a .22 caliber shell casing, a cellular phone, a small pool of blood, and some medical items left behind by the paramedics. In the diagrams the footwear impressions were color coded to indicate which subject in the scene made which impressions (Figures 13.4 to 13.6).

In this case we have the benefit of hindsight and I do not intend to be overly critical or judgmental of the first responders. They had the difficult and stressful job of securing the scene, providing aid to the victim, searching for potential armed suspects, and identifying and securing witnesses. However, had they paused for just a moment and looked over the scene, they would have concluded that the best approach into and out of the scene would have been the lawn rather than the dirt driveway on which the incident occurred and footwear impressions from the suspect were present.

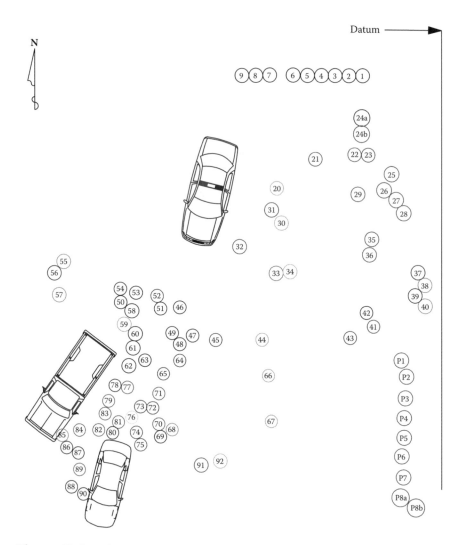

Figure 13.4 A diagram illustrating the entrance area of the scene where the suspect drove in and witnesses and first responders entered. The area immediately to the left of the vehicles is a lawn and may have been the preferred path into and out of the crime scene.

Case Number 2

Some property crime scenes, although they may not have the same intensity or priority of a personal crime, can be very extensive and elaborate. It can often take a great deal more time and effort to process a burglary scene than a death scene. This is just such a scene.

A K–12 school was broken into over summer break. The burglars approached the scene in the dirt driveway outside the auto shop, leaving tire impressions.

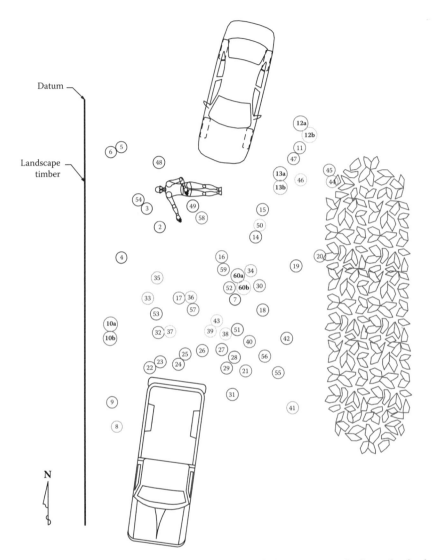

Figure 13.5 A diagram illustrating the area of the scene, including the body of the victim, and the area immediately around the body. All of the colored evidence markers represent footwear impressions, as well as markers 48, 49, and 54, which are impressions made by a Magnum boot. Marker number 7 represents a .22 caliber shell casing and markers 30 and 60a represent footwear impressions which correspond to the suspect's shoes.

They entered the school by prying open a metal door to the auto shop, leaving pry marks on the door. They walked across the shop floor, leaving footwear impressions in dust. They kicked in a door to a storage room where tools were stored, leaving a footwear impression on the door. They handled and removed tools from the storage room, leaving fingerprints. They also kicked in the door to the shop teacher's office, leaving a footwear impression on the door.

WC08-3404
Diagram #2
Legend

Baseline is landscaping timber running north and south, west of the driveway

Item #	Description	South	West
1	Victim's head	7'2"	6'
2	Red stain on dirt	10'11"	7'9"
3	Blue rescue breathing bag	9'4"	6'6"
4	Cellular phone	13'6"	4'3"
5	Red first aid kit	4'1"	4'3"
6	Plastic bag with tubing	4'6"	3'4"
7	Shell casing	17'2"	14'3"
8	Footwear impression	27'11"	3'10"
9	Footwear impression	25'10"	14'11"
10	Footwear impression	19'10"	3'5"
11	Footwear impression	4'3"	19'11"
12	Footwear impression	3'	20'2"
13	Footwear impression	7'	18'6"
14	Footwear impression	11'5"	16'
15	Footwear impression	9'6"	16'8"
16	Footwear impression	13'6"	13'1"
17	Footwear impression	17'	9'4"
18	Footwear impression	18'1"	16'8"
19	Footwear impression	14'4"	19'7"
20	Footwear impression	13'6"	21'8"
21	Footwear impression	23'3"	15'2"
22	Footwear impression	22'11"	6'9"
23	Footwear impression	22'5"	7'8"
24	Footwear impression	22'10"	8'4"
25	Footwear impression	21'11"	9'5"
26	Footwear impression	21'4"	10'4"
27	Footwear impression	21'5"	11'11"
28	Footwear impression	21'7"	12'2"
29	Footwear impression	23'	13'6"
30	Footwear impression	16'	16'3"
31	Footwear impression	25'3"	14'
32	Footwear impression	19'11"	7'6"
33	Footwear impression	17'	6'7"
34	Footwear impression	14'11"	15'2"
35	Footwear impression	15'3"	7'5"
36	Footwear impression	17'1"	9'8"
37	Footwear impression	20'	8'2"
38	Footwear impression	20'1"	13'5"
39	Footwear impression	19'10"	12'1"
40	Footwear impression	20'9"	15'6"
41	Footwear impression	26'5"	19'3"
42	Footwear impression	20'6"	18'9"
43	Footwear impression	19'7"	12'8"
44	Footwear impression	7'2"	22'9"
45	Footwear impression	6'6"	22'6"
46	Footwear impression	7'	20'
47	Footwear impression	5'	19'6"
48	Footwear impression	5'5"	7'7"
49	Footwear impression	7'11"	7'3"
50	Footwear impression	10'10"	16'5"
51	Footwear impression	20'2"	14'1"
52	Footwear impression	16'1"	14'
53	Footwear impression	18'4"	7'4"
54	Footwear impression	8'7"	5'9"
55	Footwear impression	23'5"	18'
56	Footwear impression	22'	16'10"
57	Footwear impression	17'8"	10'7"
58	Footwear impression	10'2"	11'4"
59	Footwear impression	14'7"	13'6"
60	Footwear impression	15'9"	15'

Figure 13.6 One of the legends used to describe the items of evidence within the scene and their locations. Using a legend such as this rather than placing the dimensions directly onto the diagram helps keep the diagram neat in appearance and easier to understand.

They then walked across the recently waxed gym floor, leaving foot-wear impressions. They entered the custodian's office and pried open a wall-mounted lockbox, leaving pry marks. They removed keys from the lockbox, leaving fingerprints. They entered the computer lab room and removed several recently purchased computers from their factory packaging and stole them. The computer packaging was processed for fingerprints.

They entered the office and unlocked a storage room where a large safe was stored. They pried off the safe's combination dial, leaving pry marks on the dial. They attempted to cut the hinges off the safe using power tools that they took from the shop. This left metal filings on the floor. They left the tools behind in this storage room, which were processed for fingerprints.

They used an appliance dolly from the shop to remove the safe from the storage room and wheel it into the shop. They used an acetylene torch to attempt to cut open the safe (unsuccessfully) (Figure 13.7). They handled the torch, the appliance dolly, and a fire extinguisher in the shop. They must have worked up quite a hunger because they snacked on some chips and candy, and left the wrappers behind. They also stepped on several pieces of paper in the shop, leaving footwear impressions.

On the inside window of one of the main entrance doors was a patent fingerprint in greasy perspiration. This window had been cleaned during the summer break and was likely left behind by one of the suspects (Figure 13.8).

Figure 13.7 The safe that had been removed from the office storage room and taken to the shop. The burglars unsuccessfully used an acetylene torch in an attempt to cut open the safe.

Figure 13.8 A patent fingerprint that was found on the inside window of the main entrance door. This window had been recently cleaned and this fingerprint was likely left behind by one of the burglars.

A large extensive scene such as this can take a great deal of time and effort to process. There was a lot of evidence to photograph and process for fingerprints and footwear impressions, and to collect. It took nine hours to thoroughly process this scene.

Case Number 3

A murder–suicide was the result when a woman tried to break up with her jealous lover. They had a stormy relationship that involved accusations of domestic violence against both of them, and just weeks prior to the murder there was an accusation of rape from the female victim against her boyfriend.

One night, faced with all of this, the boyfriend went to the victim's house with a .38 caliber revolver and knocked on the door. When the victim answered the door he shot her once in the chest. The bullet went through her heart, killing her in seconds. Before she fell to the floor she closed the front door. He fired another shoot through the door, missing her and going into the entertainment center and into the television set. He then immediately turned the gun on himself. He placed the muzzle of the gun in his mouth, pointing up toward the top of his head, and pulled the trigger (Figure 13.9 and Figure 13.10).

This scene was not complex in nature despite being a murder–suicide. It was photographed using overall, midrange, and close-up techniques. A scene diagram was created depicting the floor plan of the house, furniture,

Figure 13.9 The enclosed patio where the suspect shot through the open front door (pictured on the right) into the victim's chest, through the closed door into the entertainment center, and finally shot himself in the head.

Figure 13.10 The female victim laying on the floor just inside the door. Paramedics did attempt to treat the victim, but she had been shot through the heart and had died within seconds.

Figure 13.11 The victim's body on scene. Her only injury was to her chest and it was covered with a great deal of blood.

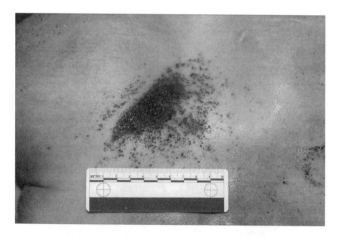

Figure 13.12 At the autopsy the victim's injury was cleaned and the stippling pattern, or burn pattern from the gunshot, is apparent. Also apparent is the area of skin that was protected by the victim's clothing. It stopped the burning material from the gunshot from contacting and burning the skin. The pathologist estimated, based on the stippling pattern, that the muzzle was only eight to ten inches from the suspect's chest when she was shot.

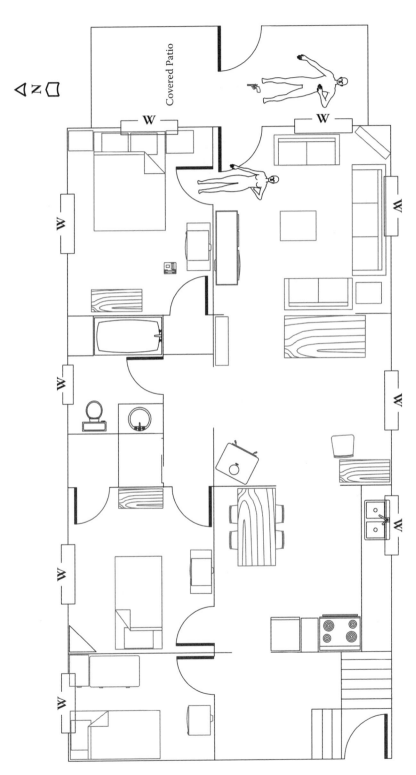

Figure 13.13 The crime scene diagram depicting the house and its contents and fixtures, the bodies, and the firearm.

Figure 13.14 A photograph showing the shot trajectory through the front door and into the entertainment center. String was run through the holes in the door and the entertainment center to illustrate the trajectory of the shot.

fixtures, and the bodies. The firearm was documented, unloaded, and collected. The trajectory of the bullet through the door and into the entertainment center was reconstructed by running string through the holes in the door and entertainment center. Last, the three spent bullets were recovered (Figures 13.11 to 13.14).

Case Number 4

A man committed suicide in the driver's seat of his car. He placed a 9-mm handgun in his mouth and fired (Figure 13.15). Upon examining the head-liner of the car at the scene, there was no blood spatter or obvious holes, cuts, or tears. There was no dent or hole in the roof of the car (Figure 13.16). The autopsy was performed the next day by a forensic pathologist. The pathologist examined the victim's skull and found a small fracture on the top left side of the skull. The pathologist did not believe that the bullet exited the top of the skull. He thoroughly examined the victim and did not find the bullet (Figure 13.17). He suggested that it was possible that the bullet impacted the skull, fractured it, and bounced back down and out of the victim's mouth. He suggested that a more thorough search of the floorboards and seats may result in the discovery of the bullet.

The vehicle, which had been stored in an indoor law enforcement impound facility, was thoroughly searched the next day. Nothing was found after a complete search of the floor, seats, and center console and dashboard.

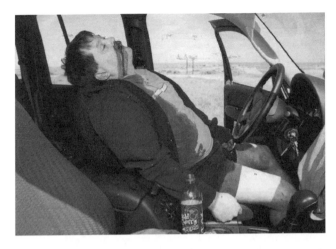

Figure 13.15 The victim shot himself in the mouth with a 9-mm handgun.

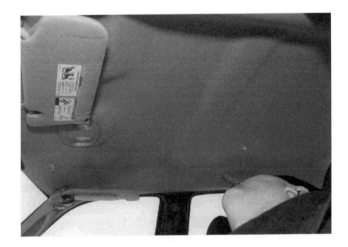

Figure 13.16 The headliner showed no signs of blood spatter from an exit wound and no impact or damage were found on the headliner at the scene.

The headliner was examined again and a very small cut was found behind the driver's seat (Figure 13.18). Approximately eighteen inches behind this small cut the bullet was found (Figure 13.19).

I contacted the coroner's office investigator on the case and informed her that I had found the bullet in the headliner of the vehicle, and the bullet had indeed exited the victim's skull. I asked if I could reexamine

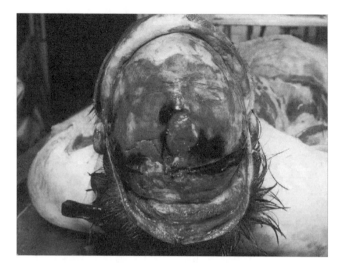

Figure 13.17 A small fracture on the top left side of the skull was documented at autopsy. The pathologist did not find the bullet in the victim's body, so the vehicle was searched again.

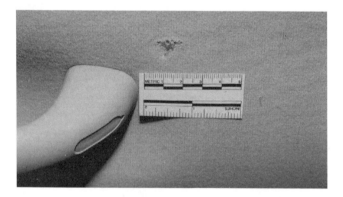

Figure 13.18 A small cut was found in the headliner above and behind the driver's seat.

the victim's body to find the undocumented exit wound on the top of the victim's head. I was informed that the body had been released to a mortuary.

I contacted the mortuary and asked if they would permit me to briefly examine the body to search for an exit wound on the head, and they consented.

Figure 13.19 Approximately eighteen inches behind that small cut the bullet was found.

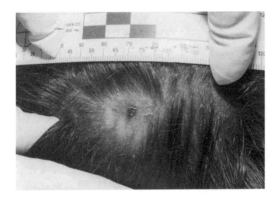

Figure 13.20 The very small exit wound on the top left side of the victim's head caused by a 9-mm bullet.

The exit wound was found. It was a very small, approximately three- or four-millimeter hole on the top left side of the head. This small hole was created by a bullet nine millimeters in width (Figure 13.20). The skin stretched, allowing the bullet to pass through without creating a large hole. There was no blood spatter on the headliner of the car, which indicated that the skin had a "squeegee" type of action on the bullet, preventing any blood from exiting the wound.

Index

A

Absorption, biological evidence, 32
Accelerants, 44–45
Accidents, video evidence, 12, *see also* Vehicles
Adhesive lint rollers, 41
Adversarial system, 125–126
AFIS, *see* Automated Fingerprint Identification System (AFIS)
Aid, rendering, 2–3
Air conditioners, 22
Anabolic steroids, 108
Animals
    blood, presumptive tests, 39
    detection of drugs, 100
    hair, trace evidence, 43
Arkansas case, sketching, 14
Arsonists, 44
Assessment of scene, 6
Automated Fingerprint Identification System (AFIS), 95
Autopsy, 118, 119
Azimuth (polar) coordinates, 20–21

B

Batteries, camera, 67
Beverages, 7, 32
Biological evidence
    absorption, 32
    collection, 34–38
    Combined DNA Indexing System, 39–40
    documentation, 34
    elimination samples, 40
    ingestion, 32
    inhalation, 31
    injection, 32
    presumptive tests, 38–39
    scene safety, 31
    searching for, 33
    sexual assault kits, 39
    trace DNA, 37–38
Biological hazards, 2, 6
Blood and bloodstains, 33
Bodily fluids, 32
Body, jurisdiction, 115–116
Booby traps, 2
Brushes, fingerprint, 91–92
Bullets, *see also* Firearms evidence; Striations
    autopsy, 118
    individual characteristics, 28, 70
Burn patterns, 44
Burnt gunpowder, 7

C

Cactus, *see* Peyote
Caliber, firearms evidence, 68–69
Cameras, *see* Photographs and photography; Video
Carpet fibers, 28, 44, *see also* Fibers
Case studies
    dairy farm murder, 127–129
    K-12 school break-in, 130–131, 133–134
    murder-suicide, 134–138
    suicide, 138–141
Casting, three-dimensional impressions, 59–61, *see also* Impression evidence
Cause of death, 114–115
Chain of custody, 24–25, 119
Check handwriting exemplar, 80
Chemicals, securing scene, 2
Chewing gum, 32
Citizens, perimeter establishment, 3
Clandestine drug labs, 2, 105
Class characteristics
    evidence, 28
    fibers, 44
Close-up photographs, 11, *see also* Photographs and photography

Clothing, *see also* Fibers
    autopsy, 118
    significance, 44
Cocaine, 101–102
CODIS, *see* Combined DNA Indexing
        System (CODIS)
Collection
    biological evidence, 34–37
    documents, 85–86
    general tips, 38
    glass, 46
    hair, 43
    live ammunition, 72
    metals and metal filings, 47
    paint, 48
    soil, 46
    trace evidence, 41
    two-dimensional impressions, 52–54
    wood, 45
Cologne, 7
Combined DNA Indexing System
        (CODIS), *see also* DNA;
        Trace DNA
    biological evidence, 39–40
Computer printers, 83–84
Consent, search and seizure, 5
Controlled substances, *see also* Plant
        material and seeds
    documentation, 99–100
    drug identification, 101–108
    field tests, 108, 110
    fundamentals, 99
    prescription drugs, 111
Copper bullet jackets, 118
Courtroom presentation and testimony
    adversarial system, 125–126
    demeanor, 123–124
    displays and exhibits, 124–125
    dress, 123–124
    fundamentals, 121
    preparation and pretrial conference,
        121–122
Courts and jurors, 9–10
Crime scene
    defined, 1
    entry log, 3
    scope, 1
Crime scene approach
    assessment of scene, 6
    crime scene defined, 1
    perimeter establishment, 3–4
    rendering aid, 2–3

    scene search, 7
    search and seizure, 4–5
    securing the scene, 1–2
CSI effect, *xiii*
Curious citizens, perimeter
        establishment, 3

D

Dairy farm murder case study, 127–129
Databases, impression evidence, 63–65
Death scene investigation
    autopsy, law enforcement role, 119
    cause of death, 114–115
    fundamentals, 113–114
    jurisdiction, body, 115–116
    manner of death, 114–115
    postmortem lividity, 116–117
    rigor mortis, 117–118
    scene documentation, 118
Deatria Doynell Hamilton v. State of
        Arkansas, 14
Demeanor in courtroom, 123–124
Dental stone, 59–61
Developing fingerprints, 91–94, *see also*
        Fingerprints
Diagrams, *see also* Sketching
    elevation, 16
    exploded, 16
    perspective, 16, 18
    shooting scene, 4
Direct evidence, 27
Directionality, floor plan, 15
Dirt, *see* Soil
Dishwashers, 7
Displays, courtroom presentation, 124–125
Distortion, crime scene
    rendering aid, 2, 3
    securing scene, 1
DNA, *see also* Combined DNA Indexing
        System (CODIS); Trace DNA
    biological fluid stain collection, 36
    collecting, 24
    CSI effect, *xiii*
    elimination samples, 40
    firearms, 75
    hair, 43
    individual characteristics, 28
    paper documents, 85–86
Documentation
    azimuth (polar) coordinates, 20–21
    biological evidence, 34

chain of custody, 24–25
controlled substances, 99–100
elevation diagram, 16
evidence collection, 23–24
exploded diagram, 16
floor plan, 15
fundamentals, 9–10
latent prints, processing, 24
legend, 15
measurement methods, 18–21
notes and reports, 21–23
perspective diagram, 16, 18
photography, 10–11
rectangular coordinates, 19
sketching, 12–14
three-dimensional impressions, 55–57
title box, 14
transecting baseline, 19–20
triangulation, 19
two-dimensional impressions, 52
video, 11–12
Documents
collection, 85–86
computer printers, 83–84
handwriting, 79–80
indented writing, 85
ink analysis, 84–85
paper analysis, 84–85
preservation, 85–86
typewriters, 80
Dogs, detection of drugs, 100
Doorknobs and doorbells
latent prints processing, 24
securing scene, 2
trace DNA, 37
Doors
notes and reports, 22
scene search, 7
Dress, courtroom appearance, 123–124
Drinking, 32
Drug identification, *see also* Manufactured
      drugs
controlled substances, 101–108
prescription drugs, 111
Dry casting, 61
Dry origin impressions, 50–51, 53–54

E

Eating, 32
Ecstasy, 105
Edited video appearance, 12

Egress points, 7, 24
Electronics (household)
notes and reports, 22
scene search, 7
Electrostatic dust lifters, 54
Elevation diagram, 16
Elimination samples
biological evidence, 40
fingerprints, 95
English *vs.* metric measures, 18
Entry points, 7, 24, *see also* Doorknobs
      and doorbells
Evidence
class characteristics, 28
collection, 23–24
defined, 27
direct evidence, 27
indirect evidence, 27–28
individual characteristics, 28–29
overlooking, scene search, 7
scene assessment, 6
unrealistic, *CSI* effect, *xiii*
Evidence, biological
absorption, 32
collection, 34–38
Combined DNA Indexing System, 39–40
documentation, 34
elimination samples, 40
ingestion, 32
inhalation, 31
injection, 32
presumptive tests, 38–39
scene safety, 31
searching for, 33
sexual assault kits, 39
trace DNA, 37–38
Evidence, firearms
bullets, 70
caliber, 68–69
gunshot residue, 74–75
handling evidence, 75–77
National Integrated Ballistics
      Information Network, 72–74
packaging evidence, 75–77
rifling, 69
safety, 67–68
shell casings, 70–72
shells, 72
shotguns, 72
understanding firearms, 68
unloading evidence, 75–77
wadding, 72

Evidence, impression
  casting, 59–61
  collecting, 52–54
  databases, 63–65
  documenting, 52, 55–57
  fundamentals, 49–50
  investigative aids, 63–65
  scale, selection, 58
  three-dimensional impressions,
    54–57, 59–61
  tire impressions, 61–62
  tool marks, 62–63
  two-dimensional impressions, 50–54
Evidence, trace
  accelerants, 44–45
  fibers, 44
  fundamentals, 41
  glass, 46
  hair, 43
  metals, 47–48
  paint, 48
  plant material and seeds, 46–47
  soil, 45–46
  wood, 45
Exhibits, courtroom, 124–125
Exploded diagram, 16
Extractor pin, 72

F

Face masks, 31, 32
Fans, 7, 22
Feet, *see* Footsteps; Footwear
Fibers
  class characteristics, 28
  trace evidence, 44
Field tests, controlled substances,
    108, 110
Fingerprints
  Automated Fingerprint Identification
    System, 95
  biological fluid stains, 34
  developing, 91–94
  firearms, 75
  fundamentals, 87–88
  individual characteristics, 28
  latent impressions, 88
  lifting, 91–94
  paper documents, 85–86
  patent impressions, 88
  photographing, 95
  plastic impressions, 90

  porous items, 97
  searching for, 90–91
Firearms evidence
  bullets, 70
  caliber, 68–69
  chain of custody example, 25
  gunshot residue, 74–75
  handling evidence, 75–77
  National Integrated Ballistics
    Information Network, 72–74
  packaging evidence, 75–77
  rifling, 69
  safety, 67–68
  scene documentation, 118
  shell casings, 70–72
  shells, 72
  shotguns, 72
  striations, 63, 70
  understanding firearms, 68
  unloading evidence, 75–77
  wadding, 72
Fire points of origin, 44
Firing pin, 72, 73
Fixtures, sketching, 14
Floor plan, 15
Flu viruses, inhalation, 31
Foods, 7, 32
Footsteps, 2
Footwear, *see also* Impression evidence
  biological fluid stains, 34
  case studies, 127–128, 131
  class characteristics, 28
  databases and investigative
    aids, 63–65
  individual characteristics, 28
Footwear, the Missed Evidence, 49
*Footwear Impression Evidence
    Detection, Recovery and
    Examination*, 49
Forged checks, 97
Fourth Amendment, U.S. Constitution, 5
Fragrance, 7
Fumes, securing scene, 2
Furniture, sketching, 14

G

Gasoline, 7, 44
Glass, 46
Gloves
  absorption, 32
  collection of evidence, 85

fingerprints, 94
ingestion, 32
trace evidence, 41
"Goat heads" example, 47
Grasses, *see* Plant material and seeds
Gunpowder, 7
Gunshot residue, 74–75

H

Hair
    greeting card, scene assessment, 6
    trace evidence, 41, 43
Handguns, *see* Firearms evidence
Handling evidence, firearms, 75–77
Handwriting, 79–80
Heaters, 22
Hepatitis B and C, 32
Heroin, 102–103
HIV, *see* Human immunodeficiency
        virus (HIV)
Human immunodeficiency virus
        (HIV), 32
Humidity, 34

I

Impression evidence, *see also* Footwear
    casting, 59–61
    collecting, 52–54
    databases, 63–65
    documenting, 52, 55–57
    fundamentals, 49–50
    investigative aids, 63–65
    latent, 88
    patent, 88
    plastic, 90
    scale, selection, 58
    three-dimensional impressions,
        54–57, 59–61
    tire impressions, 61–62
    tool marks, 62–63
    two-dimensional impressions,
        50–54
Indented writing, 85
Indirect evidence, 27–28
Individual characteristics,
        evidence, 28–29
Informal sample standards, 79
Ingestion, 32
Inhalation, 31
Injection, 32

Inks
    analysis, 84–85
    sketching, 14
Inner perimeter, establishing, 3
Investigative aids, impression evidence,
        63–65

J

Jurisdiction, body, 115–116

K

Kerosene, 44
K-12 school break-in case study, 130–131,
        133–134

L

Laminated glass, 46
Lasers, azimuth coordinates, 21
Latent prints
    collecting evidence, 24
    impressions, 88
    notes and reports, 23
    processing, 24
Latent two-dimensional impressions, 51,
        see also Impression evidence
Law enforcement role, autopsy, 119
Lead fragments, 118
Legend, 15
Lifting fingerprints, 91–94, *see also*
        Fingerprints
Lights and light switches
    notes and reports, 22
    scene search, 7
    securing scene, 2
Lines of Langer, 115
Lint rollers, adhesive, 41
Locard's exchange principle
    gunshot residue, 74
    historical development, *xiv*
    wood, 45
"London Business" text, 80
LSD (lysergic acid diethylamide), 105
Lysergic acid diethylamide (LSD), 105

M

Machinery (household), 7, 22
Magnetic fingerprint brushes, 92–93, 97
Manner of death, 114–115

Manufactured drugs, 2, *see also* Drug
     identification
Marijuana, 101, 110
MDMA (3,4-Methylenedioxymetham-
     phetamine), 105
Measurement methods
     azimuth (polar) coordinates, 20–21
     floor plans, 15
     fundamentals, 18
     rectangular coordinates, 19
     transecting baseline, 19–20
     triangulation, 19
Media, *see* Press (media)
Mescaline, 105, 108
Metals and metal filings, 41, 47–48
Methamphetamine (meth), 103–105
3,4-Methylenedioxymethamphetamine
     (MDMA), 105
Metric *vs.* English measures, 18
Midrange, location-establishing pictures,
     11, *see also* Photographs and
     photography
Murder-suicide case study, 134–138,
     see also Suicide case study
Mushrooms, 105
Music, 7, 22

N

National Guidelines for Death Investigation,
     113
National Integrated Ballistics Information
     Network (NIBIN), 72–74
Negative observations, 22–23
NIBIN, *see* National Integrated
     Ballistics Information
     Network (NIBIN)
Nonessential medical personnel,
     limiting, 3
Nonrequest samples, 79
Nose, observation with, 7
Notes
     documentation, 21–23
     photograph evidence, 10

O

Objects, moving, 2
Opium poppy, 110, *see also* Heroin
Outer perimeter, establishing, 3
Overall pictures, 10–11, *see also*
     Photographs and photography

P

Packaging evidence
     firearms evidence, 75–77
     materials used, 24
     patent impressions, 88
Paint and paint cans, 45, 48
Paper, packaging evidence, 24
Paper analysis, documents, 84–85
Paper bindles
     glass, 46
     hair, 43
     soil, 46
Pate, Shook v., 14
Patent impressions
     fingerprints, 88
     two-dimensional impressions, 52
PDR, *see Physician's Desk
     Reference (PDR)*
Perfume, 7
Perimeter establishment, 3–4
Personal information exemplar, 80
Perspective diagram, 16, 18
Petroleum products, 44
Peyote, 105, 108
Pharmacist's fold, 41
Photographs and photography,
     see also Video
     batteries, camera, 67
     biological fluid stains, 34
     documentation, 9, 10–11
     fingerprints, 95
     firearms, 76
     plastic impressions, 90
     rendering aid, 2
     safety, 67
     scale selection, 58
     scene documentation, 118
     three-dimensional impressions, 55
     tire impressions, 61
     two-dimensional impressions, 52
Physician's Desk Reference (PDR), 111
Pill finder, 111
Plant material and seeds, 46–47, *see also*
     Controlled substances
Plastic impressions, 90
Points of origin, fire, 44
Porous items, 97
Postmortem lividity, 116–117
Preparation, courtroom presentation and
     testimony, 121–122
Prescription drugs, 111

Presentation, *see* Courtroom presentation and testimony
Preservation, documents, 85–86
Press (media)
    courtroom dress, 123
    perimeter establishment, 3
Presumptive tests, 38–39
Pretrial conference, 121–122
Psilocybin (mushrooms), 105
Pubic hair, collection, 43, *see also* Sexual assault

Q

Quick Reference Guide, *xi*

R

Rectangular coordinates, 19
Rendering aid, 2–3
Reports
    documentation, 21–23
    photograph evidence, 10
Requested standards, 79
Rifling, 69, 118
Rigor mortis, 117–118

S

Safety
    firearms evidence, 67–68
    scene assessment, 6
    securing scene, 2
Saliva, 33, 35
Sawdust, 45
Scale
    selection, impression evidence, 58
    sketching, 14
    three-dimensional impressions, 55, 57
    title box, 14
Scene documentation, 118
Scene safety, 31
Scene search, 7
School break-in case study, 130–131, 133–134
Search and seizure, 4–5
Searches
    biological evidence, 33
    fingerprints, 90–91
    latent two-dimensional impressions, 51
    live ammunition, 72
    three-dimensional impressions, 54

Search warrants, 5
Securing the scene, 1–2
Seeds, *see* Plant material and seeds
Semen, 33
Semiautomatic firearms, 76
Sexual assault
    autopsy, 118
    biological evidence, 39
    chain of custody, 25
    "goat heads" example, 47
    pubic hair, collection, 43
Shell casings
    firearms evidence, 70–72
    National Integrated Ballistics Information Network, 73–74
    perimeter establishment, 4
Shells, firearms evidence, 72
Shoes, *see* Footwear
Shook v. Pate, 14
Shotguns, 72
Shrubs, *see* Plant material and seeds
Sighting devices, azimuth coordinates, 21
Sketching, 12–14, *see also* Diagrams
Smells, 7
Smoking, 32
Snow, casting impressions, 60–61
Snow print wax, 61
Soda-lime glass, 46
Soil, 45–46
Sounds, 7, 22
Spatial relationships, *see* Exploded diagram
State of Arkansas, Deatria Doynell Hamilton v., 14
Storage safe case study, 130–131, 133–134
Striations, 63, 70
Suicide case study, 138–141, *see also* Murder-suicide case study
Surveillance video, 27, *see also* Video
Swabbing, *see also* Biological evidence
    biological fluid stains, 35–37
    collection tips, 38
    elimination samples, 40
Sweat, effect on fingerprints, 88

T

TB, *see* Tuberculosis (TB)
Televisions, 7, 22
Temperature, 34, 37
Tempered glass, 46
Testimony, *see* Courtroom presentation and testimony

Threats, *see* Safety
Three-dimensional impressions
　　casting, 59–61
　　documenting, 55–57
　　fundamentals, 54–55
Three-dimensional views, *see*
　　　　Perspective diagram
Tires and tire impressions,
　　　　see also Vehicles
　　biological fluid stains, 34
　　class characteristics, 28
　　databases and investigative aids, 65
　　impression evidence, 52, 61–62
　　individual characteristics, 28
　　securing scene, 1–2
Title box, 14
Tobacco, 7, 32
Tool marks, 62–63
Trace DNA, 37–38, *see also* Combined
　　　　DNA Indexing System
　　　　(CODIS); DNA
Trace evidence
　　accelerants, 44–45
　　collecting, 24
　　fibers, 44
　　firearms, 75
　　fundamentals, 41
　　glass, 46
　　hair, 43
　　metals, 47–48
　　paint, 48
　　plant material and seeds, 46–47
　　soil, 45–46
　　wood, 45
Traffic control devices, 12
Transecting baseline, 19–20
Triangulation, 19
Trilateration, *see* Triangulation
Tuberculosis (TB), 31
Tweezers, 41, 85
Two-dimensional impressions
　　collecting, 52–54
　　documenting, 52
　　fundamentals, 50–51
Typewriters, 80

U

Understanding firearms, 68, *see also*
　　　　Firearms evidence
Undisturbed areas
　　notes and reports, 23
　　photograph evidence, 10
Unloading evidence, 75–77
Unrealistic evidence, *xiii*
Urine, 33

V

Vacuum, evidence, 41
Vaginal secretions, 33
Vandalism, 48, *see also* School break-in
　　　　case study
Vehicles, *see also* Tires and tire impressions
　　accidents, video evidence, 12
　　fingerprint searches, 90
　　glass, 46
　　latent prints processing, 24
　　paint, 48
　　plant material and seeds, 47
　　suicide case study, 138–141
　　trace DNA, 38
Video, 11–12, *see also* Photographs and
　　　　photography; Surveillance video

W

Wadding, 72
Walk through, scene assessment, 6
Walls, sketching, 14
Warrants, 5
Washing machines, 7, *see also* Electronics
　　　　(household)
Web sites, 111
Weeds, *see* Plant material and seeds
Wet origin impressions, 50, 53
Windows
　　notes and reports, 22
　　scene search, 7
　　trace DNA, 37
Wood, 45